LOOKING AFTER
YOUR PC
MADE EASY

2019 EDITION

Publisher and Creative Director: Nick Wells
Project Editor: Polly Prior
Art Director and Layout Design: Mike Spender
Digital Design and Production: Chris Herbert
Copy Editor: Daniela Nava
Proofreader: Dawn Laker
Screenshots: Roger Laing
Special thanks to Laura Bulbeck, Amanda Crook

FLAME TREE PUBLISHING
6 Melbray Mews
Fulham, London SW6 3NS
United Kingdom

Non-screenshot pictures are © 2013 Lenovo: 9b, 17t, 28, 30, 188, 190; © 2014 LG Electronics: 11b, 26; Courtesy of Dell Inc.: 16, 252;
© 2013 Toshiba Europe GmbH: 17b, 18t, 18b; © 2014 ASUS: 24, 33b, 37; © Intel Corporation: 31, 39t; © Western Digital Technologies,
Inc.: 33t; © 2014 Sony: 34, 248; © 2014 TP-Link: 35; © Copyright 2013, Misco UK Ltd: 39c; © takeMS: 39b; © 2014 Lautsprecher Teufel
GmbH: 42; © Canon (UK) Ltd 2013: 43t; Copyright © 1995-2014 SAMSUNG: 43b; Courtesy of Microsoft: 66; © 1996-2014 NETGEAR®:
125; Courtesy of MHP Computer Services Ltd 2013: 247; Courtesy of Samsung 251; and courtesy of Shutterstock.com and the following
contributors: Monkey Business Images: 1; RomboStudio: 3; Africa Studio: 4 & 14; Gorvik: 5t & 46; wongwean: 5b & 90; Christian Delbert:
6b & 164; frank_peters: 6t & 122; gcpics: 7b & 208; SOMMAI: 7t & 186; Melpomene: 9t; George Dolgikh: 41; Andresr: 57t; improvise:
62r; Pressmaster: 78t; violetkaipa: 79; tokyoimagegroups: 80; Dasha Petrenko: 87; Konstantin Chagin: 94t; rangizzz: 105t; Andrey_Popov:
108; antos777: 192b; Ldprod: 196; Davooda: 197–98; Barabasa: 206t; Telnov Oleksii: 221; GVictoria: 224; DVARG: 232; cunaplus:
238; Venus Angel: 239t; Sinisa Botas: 249; JJ Studio: 250.

ISBN 978-1-78755-722-2

Manufactured in China

1 3 5 7 9 10 8 6 4 2

LOOKING AFTER
YOUR PC
MADE EASY

2019 EDITION

ROGER LAING

FLAME TREE
PUBLISHING

CONTENTS

There are now so many types of computer – desktop, laptop, notebook, ultrabook, tablet – that picking the right one can be quite bewildering. This chapter will not only help you choose your perfect PC, but will also guide you through the various parts of the computer system. You'll learn how to connect the different components and add peripheral devices, such as speakers or printers.

GETTING STARTED 46

For your computer to function, you will need an operating system, which for most PCs is a version of Microsoft Windows. This chapter explains how to use Windows, from accessing your PC's core functions through the Start screen to organizing and storing your files and folders on the desktop. It shows you how you can use Windows apps to do everything, from playing music to organizing photos.

PUTTING YOUR PC TO WORK. 90

In this chapter, you will put your PC through its paces, by learning how you can use it to surf the internet, send email, chat online, store photos, record and edit video, search for and play music, access top movies and hit TV shows and connect with friends, family and colleagues through social media. You will also see how it can be used to write letters, create presentations and manage your finances.

NETWORKS

It's now essential to have a home network to access the internet, connect to the printer and to share files or play games across PCs. This chapter will cut through the confusion and explain exactly what a network is, and show you how to set one up, so that wherever you are in the house, you can share files, media and even a printer.

PROTECTION

Your PC is chock full of personal data that you don't want to lose or anyone else to get hold of. In order to protect your PC, you need to back up regularly and guard against viruses and other malware. This chapter will guide you through the best ways of doing this, and also show you how to set up family safety controls so you can keep your children safe online – and regulate which apps they can use and for how long!

TOUCH

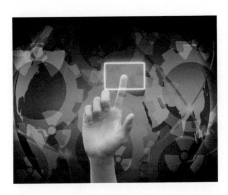

Windows 10 was designed to work across PCs, tablets and smartphones, and this chapter takes a look at the different types of touch screen PCs, showing you how you can control your device by touching or tapping rather than using the mouse. From built-in apps like Microsoft OneNote to special versions of desktop programs with touch, there are many apps designed to let you do more with touch on your tablet PC.

TROUBLESHOOTING & MAINTENANCE

Like any human, computers aren't always at their best, and when things go wrong, as this chapter shows, there are steps you can take to identify the problems and fix them. It will guide you through some simple – and effective – maintenance tips to help avoid problems and make your computer perform better. It will also show you how to bring a new lease of life to your computer by adding to or upgrading your hardware.

INTRODUCTION

We increasingly rely on computers – at work and at home – to organize our life. The PC looks after us, but who looks after the PC? You can, with the help of this book. It contains all the essential information to help you set up and run a PC, together with the fixes needed when things, inevitably, go wrong.

EVERYTHING YOU NEED TO KNOW

Whether it's just keeping a calendar, staying in touch with friends, planning the family budget or any of the millions of other tasks that you can accomplish with a PC, you switch it on and expect it to work. Most of the time it will but, not surprisingly given the advanced technology

Above: The very modern look of the Windows 10 Start screen.

inside every machine, it is sometimes very sluggish, crashes or – worse – won't start at all.

Ask a specialist and they'll rattle off all sorts of technical jargon – from RAM to bus speeds – which can be very confusing. That's where this book comes in. It will explain simply and clearly what each term means. It will guide you through the often bewildering choice of hardware, software and add-ons that are available, so that you end up with the PC that best meets your requirements. You will also discover the simple techniques needed to keep your PC running smoothly and, if disaster strikes, how to troubleshoot problems and fix them.

TAP OR CLICK?

While the book focuses on Microsoft's latest operating system, Windows 10, most actions carried out in desktop mode apply equally to earlier versions of Windows. Any major changes are highlighted. Although Windows is now designed for touch, most actions can be done as easily with the traditional keyboard or mouse; where the text says click, you can tap instead if you have a touch screen. Chapter Six shows how different touch gestures correspond to using the mouse.

Above: The more traditional look of Windows in Desktop mode.

BITE-SIZE INFORMATION

As a practical guide to looking after your PC, you don't need to read this book from cover to cover. It is organized so that you can dip into the different areas that are relevant to you, whether that's how to use the touch gestures in Windows, what to consider when buying a new PC or how to check if a virus is slowing down your computer.

Each section stands alone and includes simple guides for tasks that you can do. For example, in one section you will learn how to free up memory to improve performance, while in another you can follow the instructions to add more physical memory to your PC and speed it up.

STEP-BY-STEP

Throughout the book, step-by-step guides take you through the exact actions you need to follow. They cover topics such as installing Windows, how to clean up your hard drive, and quick ways to share your photos and other files online. Each section gives clear, concise instructions on what to do, as well as hot tips to make the tasks easier.

HELP!

In the unlikely event you do get really stuck on a particular topic, we're here to help. Simply email your query to Flame Tree

Above: Later on, you will learn how to import pictures to your computer and share them online.

Publishing at support@flametreepublishing.com. While we cannot operate a 24-hour helpline to cover the complete range of PC problems, we will respond by email as soon as possible.

YOUR GUIDE

If you have never looked after a PC before, this book will get you up and running as quickly as possible. Author Roger Laing will introduce you to a broad range of features in order to give you a deeper understanding of the PC and how to do more with it – so you'll soon be using your computer like a pro.

SEVEN CHAPTERS

In seven chapters, this book will take you through the essentials of looking after your PC.

Above: This book will guide you through the various menus and settings on your PC.

Chapter One will show you how to set up your machine, which types to choose (e.g. desktop or tablet PC), the hardware options to consider and how to connect everything so it runs smoothly. Chapter Two will get you started: from installing or upgrading the operating system to navigating your way effortlessly through the Modern look of Windows or the traditional desktop.

Chapter Three is all about putting your PC to work and choosing the software that's right for you. It tackles how to find the programs and install, upgrade or remove them, as well as how to get the most from the apps that come with Windows. This is where to go if you want to learn the trouble-free ways to set up your PC, show photos, watch TV, play videos, manage your music or go social. Here, you can also find out about adding the tools needed to organize your documents, mail and as much of your work and personal life as you choose.

Chapter Four is all about networking. Discover the tricks of setting up your home network so you can share information with others inside your house or outside, via the internet, including backing up and syncing your files with cloud services. Chapter Five will show the precautions to take so that you – and your personal information – are safe online. It outlines how to physically protect your PC (from virus attack or snoopers), as well as how to use backup and recovery to make sure that you never lose that vital file or irreplaceable picture.

Chapter Six shows how to use the new breed of 'hybrid' laptops that are part PC and part touch screen, and how to make the most of the new touch features in Windows. Chapter Seven will look at what you can do when things go wrong. The troubleshooting guide

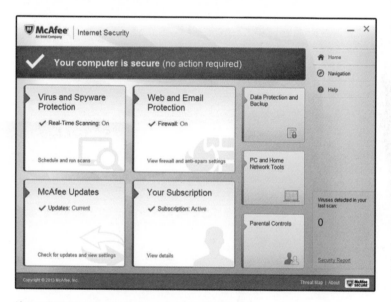

Above: Chapter Five will show you how to keep your PC protected.

runs through the quick and easy as well as advanced fixes for problems with your PC, programs, screen, sound, batteries and more. It also covers the routine maintenance that can prevent trouble and the hardware upgrades that can turbocharge your PC for a new lease of life.

HOT TIPS AND SHORTCUTS

All through the book, Hot Tips provide quick and handy information on the way to get more from your PC. They also highlight many shortcuts and quick techniques, which will help you to become an expert user.

BUYING A PC

There are so many different types of computer that picking one can be quite bewildering. The choices become clearer if you decide what you really want the PC for: working on documents, social networking, gaming or watching the latest videos, for example.

WHICH TYPE OF PC?

PCs come in all shapes and sizes, from the traditional desktop or tower PC to the all-in-one or laptop.

Tower PCs

These big rectangular boxes are what first springs to mind when you think of PCs. Readily available, they offer the widest number of options for adding extras, from TV tuner to card reader. They also have several ports for connecting monitors, printers, sound systems and the like. Due to their bulk, they do take up space and are generally noisier than other types of computer.

Above: Tower PCs take up more space than other types of PC.

All-in-one PCs

Great if you're not a fan of cables, as the monitor and computer bits are all in one unit. They only take up the

> ## Hot Tip
> Most all-in-one PCs have touch screens in order to take advantage of the touch features in Windows. Look for 10-point touch, as that allows you to use both hands.

same space as the monitor itself but don't have as many ports for connections and are not easily upgradeable.

Laptop PCs

Above: All-in-one PCs are great for those who don't like cables.

They are known by a variety of names and vary greatly in size of screen – from 7 to 17 in (17–43 cm) – and power. The one common factor is that they are light enough to be carried around and can work off a battery for several hours before needing to be recharged. As with the all-in-one, they generally have a limited number of ports, aren't easily upgradeable and have a trackpad/touchpad instead of a mouse.

Netbook

Their screen size is quite small (10–12 in/25–30 cm) and they are generally inexpensive systems that have evolved from mini laptops. They are primarily useful for browsing and working online.

Left: Netbooks are most useful for using the internet.

Ultrabooks

Ultrabooks are the newest thing in the laptop world and are rapidly taking over. Introduced by Intel, the processor manufacturer, these ultraportables have to meet the following specifications:

Above: Wafer-thin Ultrabooks are an exciting new development.

⚬ **Wafer Thin:** They have to be wafer thin, use a low voltage Intel core processor, have at least five hours of battery life between charges and boot up in seconds.

⚬ **Touch Screens:** With the arrival of Windows 10 and touch, they also feature touch screens, so many models will also convert to tablets.

Notebooks

Although ultraportables may be taking over, there is still room for notebooks: the larger laptops that provide all you need for an everyday PC and desktop replacement. These typically have a 14 in (35 cm) screen or larger. Notebooks usually offer more storage and a wider range of features. As a result, they are not as readily portable as other types.

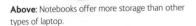

Above: Notebooks offer more storage than other types of laptop.

Tablet PCs

Essentially, these are PCs that can operate as a normal laptop, but have a touch screen that can slide, flip or be detached to work as a tablet. You navigate around the screen using your finger and type in text by tapping the on-screen keyboard. In tablet mode, you can take advantage of the touch features in Windows, while laptop mode provides a regular keyboard for heavy text work. The downside is that a reasonable laptop screen size can make for an oversized tablet.

Above: Tablet PCs can be navigated using the touch screen and have an on-screen keyboard.

WHAT YOU'LL NEED FOR ... WORK

Everyday tasks, like checking emails or browsing the web, are easily done on budget computers, but for typing that long report or putting together a presentation, you'll want a powerhouse PC.

Hot Tip

Instead of your fingers doing the tapping, you can use a stylus, also called a digital pen, to control your PC by touch.

Desktop

These are the essential ingredients your desktop PC needs for work requirements:

- **Keyboard and mouse:** Although often overlooked, as the main contact point between you and your PC, it pays to make sure they are right for you. Consider wireless versions if you don't like cables.

- **Processors:** Still largely a choice between AMD and Intel. A budget processor is fine for most work-related tasks. You only need to go for the faster models if you are planning to use your computer for heavy tasks.

Above: Webcams are a key piece of equipment for enabling web conferences.

- **Hard drive:** Although it's surprising how big some Word files get, a 250–500 GB drive is sufficient for most.

- **Webcam:** An essential these days, whether it's for connecting with family or friends, or a web conference with colleagues.

Laptop

These are the essential ingredients your laptop needs for work requirements:

- **Graphics:** New processors come with a graphics card built in, which is suitable for most work purposes, unless you use design or CAD programs.

- **Batteries:** With new laptops you may have a choice of 3-, 6-, 9- or 12-cell battery packs. The bigger the pack, the longer it lasts, but the heavier it is.

- **Processor:** If you're only using the laptop for basic daily tasks, such as checking emails, there is no need to pay for the latest, most powerful chip.

- **Display:** If you do a lot of figure work or plan to use the laptop as a desktop replacement, go for the largest screen size possible. Otherwise it's a question of personal preference.

- **Optical drives:** Still useful for installing software and storing or sharing files, for example if you're travelling and there's no good internet connection.

WHAT YOU'LL NEED FOR ... LEISURE

Whether it's getting the news from around the world, or watching a live sporting event or the latest movie, the PC is taking over from TV as our entertainment centre.

Desktop

These are the essential ingredients your desktop PC needs for leisure requirements:

- **Blu-ray drives**: These are now more affordable and support high-definition (HD) films that will show up well on a big PC screen.

- **Processor**: You want a powerful processor for smooth playback of your videos and music.

- **Display**: The larger the better – for example, a 23- or 24-in (58–60 cm) full HD monitor – if it's going to be your replacement TV.

Above: It's easy to watch the latest movies on a PC.

- **Hard drive**: Choose one with the space (from 500 GB to 2 TB) to store all your big music and movie files.

Laptop

These are the essential ingredients your laptop needs for leisure requirements:

- **Optical drives**: Good to have if you have an extensive DVD/CD collection of music and videos, although fewer laptops have optical drives now, as more people use the new online cloud services.

Hot Tip

For a blockbuster experience when watching movies, add a stereo set that includes a separate bass speaker (also called a subwoofer).

○ **Graphics**: A separate graphics processing system is a must for watching movies or editing video.

○ **Processor**: Each generation of chip offers better performance and greater power efficiency, so it is worth going for the best, most affordable option.

○ **Display**: The extra weight of a larger screen is worth it if it makes for a better viewing experience.

○ **Batteries**: There's always a compromise between portability and the extra weight of carrying around additional batteries. However, the batteries on most mainstream laptops will last a minimum of four hours – enough to see the movie through to the end.

Above: Many people use cloud online services to store music collections.

WHAT YOU'LL NEED FOR ... PLAY

There are many competing devices available for gamers – from iPad to Xbox – but when it comes to power and speed, the PC is hard to match.

Desktop

Set your desktop up with these and your play will never be the same again:

○ **Processor**: Although you'll pay a premium for the most powerful chips, such as the Intel Core i9-9900K, you'll see the difference in faster, smoother game play.

○ **Graphics**: The most important choice when it comes to gaming is that you need a dedicated graphics processor rather than an integrated one.

- **Speaker system**: Go for the surround sound option so that you'll be, literally, at the centre of the action.

- **Display**: For blur-free action, look for a monitor that has fast response times. You also want good colour reproduction and wide viewing angles for multi player games.

Laptop

Kit your laptop up with these for a truly fantastic gaming experience:

- **Lightness is all**: Newer models are unlikely to have an optical drive, so you'll have to download your games or play online.

- **Graphics**: Go for a separate graphics processing system, which is great for 3-D games, rather than an integrated one.

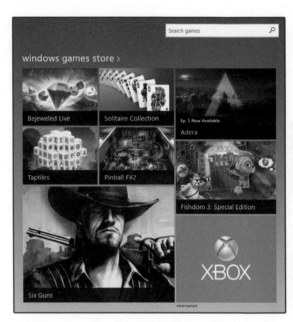

Above: Newer laptop models may not have an optical drive, meaning games will have to be downloaded or played online.

- **Processor**: The faster the better.

- **Display**: The bigger the display, the better, although it adds to the weight. Consider connecting your laptop to a desktop monitor when not on the go to get the best of both worlds.

- **Batteries**: Faster processor, bigger screen, separate graphics system – they all eat up your battery power. Consider models that can use swappable or snap-on battery packs.

Hot Tip

Going for a top-of-the-range processor will also extend the life of your laptop, as future versions of your favourite games are always going to need more power.

GET TO KNOW YOUR PC

Despite attempts to jazz them up, most PCs look pretty box-like. Here's a guide to the main parts of the computer system.

WHAT MAKES A PC?

Although all-in-one computers are sought after as entertainment PCs, the traditional PC with a separate base unit still has its place.

Computer Case

This holds the main PC components and is also known as the system unit or base unit. These PC shells come in a variety of shapes, sizes, colours and styles.

Types of Case

These are the main types of computer case:

- **Tower**: High and deep, this was once the most common type of case. Generally, too big to go on the desk, they sit on the floor.

- **Mini tower**: A more compact version of the tower, it can squeeze on to the desktop or sit on the floor.

- **Desktop**: Rectangular box that sits flat on the desktop, usually with the monitor on top.

- **Mini desktop**: A space saver that can be tucked away in a corner of the desktop.

Above: Mini desktop computer case.

- **All-in-one**: Screen and computer components are all together in a single unit.

Monitor

Also known as a video display, this is the screen where information from the computer is displayed. These are its other attributes:

- **Screen size**: Measured across the diagonal, like TVs.

- **Resolution**: In order to create an image on the screen, monitors light up small dots called pixels. The more pixels packed into the screen space, the higher the resolution and the clearer the image will appear. Resolution is shown as a figure, e.g. 1920 x 1080, which is 1920 pixels wide and 1080 pixels high.

Above: It is possible to alter the resolution of the screen for a clearer image.

- **Aspect ratio**: It is important to avoid distortion when resizing images or videos for showing on different-size monitors. On traditional monitors, the standard was 4:3, i.e. four units wide to three units high, whereas for high definition (HD) widescreen monitors it is 16:9, and changes again with Ultra HD/4K.

- **Controls**: Generally, the only one in frequent use is the power button.

○ **Built-in extras**: A webcam and integrated stereo speakers, for example, are handy if you regularly use video chat.

○ **Types of monitor**: Although they are all likely to be LCD (liquid crystal display, also known as flat panel), there's more than one type of panel. IPS (In-Plane Switching) gives the best display and viewing angles, but is expensive. Vertical Alignment (VA) panels are good and reasonably priced, while the majority of screens use the relatively inexpensive Twisted Nematic (TN) technology. Organic light-emitting diode (OLED) is the latest visual display technology, used particularly in high-end tablets.

○ **Energy-efficient displays**: Look for monitors that are marked 'LED backlight'.

Touch-screen Monitors

Multi-touch monitors are measured by the number of separate touches that they can read simultaneously. For example, a 10-point multi-touch monitor can recognize the separate touch of all 10 fingers on your hands.

Windows 8.1 was the first operating system designed for

Above: Multi-touch monitors can recognize multiple finger touches at the same time.

touch screens. For a monitor to work fully with Windows, it has to be able to react to at least five simultaneous touch points.

Keyboard

Using a keyboard is still the easiest way to input letters and figures into documents. With keyboard shortcuts, you can also action commands for the computer to follow, such as pressing the Alt + Tab key to cycle through the open programs.

Modern keyboards connect to the PC via a USB port rather than the previous keyboard connector. Consider a wireless keyboard if you don't want the clutter of cables. Touch screens have an on-screen keyboard to enter information.

Mouse

If you don't have a touch screen and can't use gestures to control your PC, you'll need a mouse. As well as acting as on-screen pointer, the mouse has a number of buttons or wheels that can be clicked or pushed to access menus, scroll pages, and so on. Just as with the keyboard, mice connect via USB cable rather than a dedicated port. Wireless mice offer more flexibility for moving around your physical desktop.

Hot Tip
One useful shortcut is pressing the Print Screen (PrtSc) key to capture an image of what's on your display. You can then paste it into programs such as Paint or Word to save.

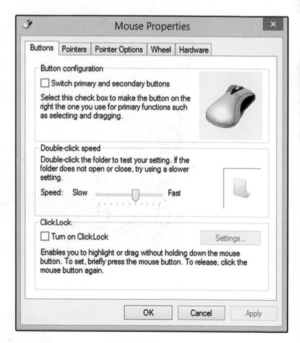

Above: A mouse can be connected via a USB cable, though wireless mice are also available.

PC: EXTERNAL

Although every PC model is different in its design and layout, many of the same features are always included; here's a guide to what to expect. We have labelled what can be seen here.

Built-in webcam

Below: The different features visible of an all-in-one PC.

USB connector

Headphone connector

Microphone connector

USB connector

3

5 Optical drive bay

4

Memory card reader

Monitor controls

1

Power button

2

Activity lights

FRONT

1 Power button
For switching the machine on and off.

2 Activity lights
They glow when the computer is on, with the hard drive light flickering when it's in action.

3 Connectors
With some of the more frequently used connections, such as headphones, microphone and USB devices.

4 Memory card reader
For reading different media cards, such as those used for transferring photos from your camera.

5 Optical drive bays
These slots hold optical drives, which may be CD, DVD or Blu-ray players.

REAR (see page 30)

1 Power button/cable
The one essential without which nothing works.

Voltage switch
If you move country, use this to change to the power frequency of your new location.

2 Air vent/Fan
Essential for dissipating the heat created by the PC. It's a good idea to clean the fan and vents occasionally so that they work more efficiently.

Keyboard/mouse ports
You may have these ports for plugging in the keyboard or mouse, although most use USB connections now.

3 Network port
For connecting the Ethernet cable that links you to the internet or home network.

4 USB ports
For plugging in USB devices, such as keyboard, mouse, printer, webcam or external drive.

Hot Tip
Fast USB 3.0 ports, which have transfer speeds up to 20 times quicker than USB 2.0, are coloured blue.

Air vent | Power button | TV tuner connector | Network port | HDMI-IN connector for linking to a DVD player, games console | HDMI-OUT connector to add a second screen

4 USB ports

Above: The different features visible from the rear of an all-in-one desktop PC.

Sound ports

For connecting various sound devices, such as external speakers, which may plug into the Line Out (green colour) or USB port. There may also be a microphone port at the back (as well as or instead of the front), which is pink.

Monitor ports

Connect the PC to an external display.

Wi-Fi antenna

For accessing a wireless network.

5 TV tuner

To get all your favourite programmes on the PC. The TV adapter fits into one of the expansion slots.

PC: INTERNAL

Most of the advanced technology that does all the clever things which are possible
with a PC is kept out of sight, inside the computer itself.

Power Supply

The transformer converts the mains supply into a voltage that the PC
can use; cables from this supply power to the rest of the system.

System Board

Also known as the motherboard, this houses many of the
computer's other components, including the processor, memory and
expansion slots. It also houses the chipset, which is the way various
components communicate with the CPU (central processing unit).
On the chipset are a series of chips that control basic computer
operations, such as keyboard, mouse, networking, sound, and so on.
The chipset can't be changed or replaced.

Above: Intel Core processor.

Processor

Technically known as the central processing unit (or CPU), the faster and more powerful it is,
the better. The two main manufacturers of processors are Intel and AMD. The first part of a
processor's name shows the family to which it belongs: for Intel, that is currently Core (previously
it was Pentium) and for AMD, it is Ryzen. The name is followed by the number of cores and model
number, such as i9-9900K for Intel or 7 1800x for AMD. Generally, the higher the number, the
more powerful a processor.

The main measure of a processor is its speed, sometimes referred to as its clock speed. Each
tick of the clock – or cycle – the processor does something, such as a mathematical calculation
or moving data in and out of memory. The more cycles a second, the faster the PC. Processor
speeds are shown in gigahertz (GHz), so a 4.0 GHz processor does 4 billion cycles a second.
The minimum required for Windows is 1 GHz.

Above: Websites such as BBC iPlayer allow you to catch up with TV programmes on your PC.

Processor cache memory is where the CPU temporarily stores data it works with frequently. Measured in megabytes (MB), the bigger the memory cache, the better the performance.

> ## Hot Tip
> Even if you don't have a TV tuner, websites like BBC iPlayer make it possible to watch TV on your PC via the internet.

Memory

Random Access Memory (or RAM) is the workspace of your PC. When the machine is switched on, it temporarily stores part of the operating system, as well as any applications or files you're using.

> ## Hot Tip
> As RAM is wiped clean when the power is switched off, you have to save information stored in memory to the hard drive if you want to keep it.

You need about 4 GB if you want to run several programs at once – such as streaming your music while writing an email – without slowing things down. For more demanding activities, 8 GB or more is desirable.

Storage

The hard drive is where the PC stores all your files, images and the like. 1 GB of RAM stores around 250 MP3 songs, 200 photos (average size 5 MB) or one full-length movie. By the time you move up to a 1 TB drive that's 250,000 songs, 200,000 photos or 1,000 movies. Most stand-alone PCs have from 500 GB drives up to 1 or 2 TB.

The performance of a drive depends on how quickly it transfers data, which is measured in gigabits per second (Gbps); the higher the number, the better. Performance also depends on how fast the drives spin. Typically, SATA hard drives spin at 7,200 revolutions per minute (rpm), although there are more expensive ones available that go at 10,000 rpm.

Graphics Card

Also known as a video card, video adapter or display adapter, this expansion card slots into a section reserved for cards that 'expand' the capabilities of the PC.

Above: A large amount of data can be stored on a 1TB hard drive.

The card controls how good things look on your monitor, which is a feature of the number of colours available (colour depth) and the number of pixels (resolution). Each pixel (that is, picture element) is made up of a red, green and blue element, which is adjusted to produce a specific colour.

The resolution measures the number of pixels on screen, such as 1920 x 1080, which means that the screen image is displayed using 1920 pixel rows and 1080 columns.

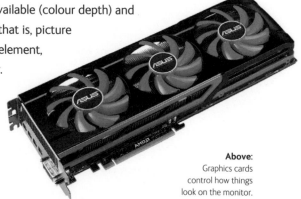

Above: Graphics cards control how things look on the monitor.

Sound Card

Every PC has a sound card embedded into the system board (also known as the motherboard). This onboard audio doesn't deliver the same sound quality as a dedicated sound card.

For serious music listening or game play, add a sound card in one of the expansion card slots to improve audio quality or offer extra features, such as special support for surround sound.

Optical Drive

This is a general term that covers CD, DVD and the latest Blu-ray drives. They are optical, as they use laser light to read and write data to the discs. The drives enable you to play music, watch movies, install programs and copy or back up data.

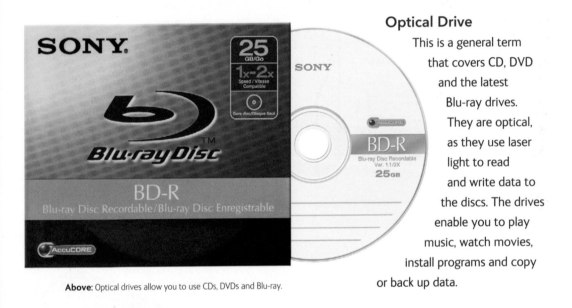

Above: Optical drives allow you to use CDs, DVDs and Blu-ray.

Each type of drive has versions for read-only, read and write (once), or read and rewrite (record on the discs several times).

The best guide to performance is the speed with which it completes these tasks, which is measured relative to the base speed of playing an audio CD. For example, if a drive has a read speed of 48x, it means that it reads data 48 times faster than a music CD player. The three speed measures are write speed, rewrite speed and read speed, and are often shown in that order.

Memory Card Reader

These are handy for transferring photos, music and video files from digital cameras, smartphones and the like. Most readers support several formats, such as Secure Digital (SD), MultiMedia Card (MMC) or CompactFlash (CF).

Ethernet Connector

This is a high-speed cable connection for linking your PC to your home network or to a router to connect to the internet. Technically known as the Network Interface Controller or Card (NIC), it is also referred to as an Ethernet card or network adapter.

Ethernet provides a faster connection than wireless, with many PCs supporting Gigabit Ethernet, which offers speeds up to 1,000 megabits per second (Mbps).

Wireless Card

Wireless cards are usually pre-installed into one of the expansion slots inside the computer. Typically, the back of the adapter enables you to screw in or attach an antenna to get a better signal.

Hot Tip
Set your screen to a higher resolution to make items appear sharper and smaller. At lower resolutions there are fewer items, but they are larger and easier to see.

Above: An antenna can be added to a wireless card to help get a better signal.

GET TO KNOW YOUR LAPTOP

The days of the barely luggable laptop have long gone and, with the huge variety in size and function, there's a model to suit every lifestyle.

LAPTOP: EXTERNAL

Portable computers are the best example of the all-in-one PC and how you can cram highly sophisticated technology into a very small space.

1 Screen

Typically, laptops have a resolution of 1366 x 768 pixels. If you can, go for models that support a higher resolution, such as 1600 x 900 or the full HD effect: 1920 x 1080. Touch screens are good if you want to get the most out of Windows.

2 Webcam

The small hole at the top of the laptop screen is a camera that can take still images and video – particularly useful for video chat or web conferences.

Microphone

The built-in microphone isn't broadcast quality, but will get your message across.

Hot Tip

If your laptop doesn't have a webcam, you can get one that plugs into the USB port and sits on top of the screen lid.

Speakers

They have to be small to fit in, so the sound quality isn't great, particularly for music, which is why all laptops also have a headphones port.

Webcam
2

Screen
1

Start

Left: Various
external features
of a laptop PC.

Keyboard
3

Monitor port
to connect to a
larger display.

HDMI port for video
and audio connection,
such as to a TV.

7
Headphones
socket

5
USB
3.0 port

Air vent

6
Memory
card reader

4
Touchpad

3 Keyboard

Although it is the part of the laptop with which you have the most contact, the keyboard
doesn't always get the attention it deserves. A good keyboard should have:

- frequently used buttons, such as Delete, larger than the rest
- curved keys to help prevent errors
- a reasonable gap between keys
- long palm rest, which supports the wrist and helps to prevent strain.

4 Touchpad

Also known as a trackpad, this is in effect your mouse. Make sure it's not too sensitive to the touch, with the cursor hard to control and skipping all over.

5 USB port

Your laptop will have one or more USB ports that let you plug devices – from hard drives to printers and speakers – into it without having to switch off or go through any complex set-up. Newer laptops may have the blue-coloured USB 3.0 (also called SuperSpeed USB) port.

Above: Change how the trackpad responds in Mouse Properties in the Control Panel.

Network port
The Ethernet or network port lets you connect your laptop to a wired network.

PC card slot
Older laptops may have a PC card slot, which can provide additional features, such as wireless connectivity.

6 Memory card reader
This is used for transferring files, via media card, from camera, smartphone or other gizmos.

7 Headphones socket
When you've had enough of the tinny noise that comes from built-in speakers, plug your headphones in.

LAPTOP: INTERNAL

System Board

This is also known as the motherboard or mainboard. Unlike desktop PCs, all parts inside a laptop are connected to this system board.

Processor

Known as the Central Processing Unit (CPU), this controls your laptop, executing the commands to launch Word, play a video, etc. Your laptop may have a single CPU, two (known as dual-core) or four, which has four processors in one package.

All CPUs have a clock speed measured in gigahertz per second (GHz) – the faster the better.

Above: Central Processing Units control your laptop.

Memory

The more memory installed, the more you can do. If you have the choice, opt for the 64-bit version of Windows, as this allow you to use 4 GB or more of memory. The 32-bit versions only recognize up to about 3.89 GB of memory.

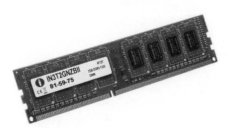

Above: DDR3 memory is still popular despite the advent of DDR4.

Memory comes in two types: DDR3 and DDR4. The latter is faster and has much greater memory capacity than earlier versions, while using less power.

Storage

For the sake of lightness, hard drives on laptops tend to have much smaller capacities than desktop versions, particularly the new Ultrabooks. Ideally, you want at least 250 GB.

Above: Solid State hard drives are very power efficient.

Graphics Card

There are two types of graphics card: integrated and discrete.

- **Integrated**: This shares the system memory and is fine for most tasks, like surfing the web or playing video.

- **Discrete**: This is a separate card which has its own dedicated memory, so it doesn't consume any processing power, making it better for playing the more demanding games.

Wireless Card

Internal cards, pre-installed by the manufacturer, are convenient because they don't use one of the few ports you have on the laptop. The downside is that, as Wi-Fi standards change, they may not support the latest and fastest connections.

Above: Internal wireless cards make it simple to connect to networks.

Bluetooth

Bluetooth is a good way to connect to mobile devices, such as smartphones and tablets, as well as add-ons like external speakers.

Optical Drive

As it adds to the weight, most laptops are sold without optical drives. The expectation is that software, games and files will all be downloaded from online services.

GETTING IT ALL CONNECTED

Whatever type of PC you have, there's work to be done in connecting the different components or adding peripheral devices, such as speakers or printers.

PUTTING YOUR PC TOGETHER

Whether you're only upgrading part of your system or have gone for components from different manufacturers, it can be challenging.

Connecting Your Monitor

Any of the following can be used to connect your monitor to your PC:

- **VGA**: The oldest type of connection, with a D-shape connection.

- **DVI**: White, rectangular connector with a series of pins that connects an LCD monitor to your PC.

Hot Tip
If your PC and monitor have different connector ports, there are adapters that can be fitted to the cables, such as converting a DVI to a VGA adapter.

Above: Various components can be connected to your computer.

- **HDMI**: It lets you connect your PC to a high-definition TV or monitor and provides the best quality connection. It is particularly appealing for gamers.

Connecting a Touch-screen Monitor

In addition to using one of the connectors above, a USB cable has to connect the screen to the system unit, in order to interpret the touch signals.

PC Speakers

Unless speakers are integrated into the monitor, you will need to add your own; here are some options:

- **Stereo set**: The basic pair of a left and right speaker.

- **2.1**: The 2 is a pair of speakers, while the 1 is a subwoofer that adds richer bass sounds.

- **Surround sound**: Geared towards gamers, this has a stereo pair of speakers, a subwoofer, a central speaker for dialogue in movies and several satellite speakers for sounds around and behind you.

Connecting Your Speakers

Typically, on a stand-alone PC, the speakers will connect via the Line In port at the back. Some speakers draw their power through the USB port rather than having a separate power lead.

Above: Surround-sound speakers are perfect for immersing yourself in a game.

Connecting Keyboard and Mouse

Usually, these connect through the ubiquitous USB port. On older models, there may be dedicated connectors – green for the mouse and purple for the keyboard – that plug into the correspondingly coloured ports at the back of the PC.

ADDING A PRINTER

Now you have got your PC together, you'll want a printer to output a hard copy of your documents or photos.

Choosing a Printer

You can choose from the following types of printer:

- **Inkjet printers**: These are the most popular. They work by spraying different-coloured inks on to the paper. Lasers fuse toner powder onto the paper and can handle higher volumes of printing, but are more expensive. Inkjet printers are inexpensive, but the replacement ink cartridges are costly. High-end inkjets will print more pages more quickly.

- **Laser printers**: These are more expensive to buy, as are the toner cartridges they use, but they print substantially more pages than inkjets before they need to be replaced.

- **All-in-one printers**: These combine a printer with a scanner, copier and, in some cases, fax machine. Handy space savers, they remove the need for separate machines and finding spare ports to connect them.

Connecting the Printer

Most printers connect directly to the PC via a USB port. Once connected, Windows should automatically install the printer software so that you can get printing straightaway.

Above: Inkjet printers are reasonably inexpensive.

Above: Laser printer toner cartridges need replacing less often.

You can also connect to the printer by wireless or wired network (*see* pages 145–147), or locally by Bluetooth if available.

CONNECTING VIA BLUETOOTH

Probably the only technology to be named after a Viking king, Bluetooth lets you create a short-range wireless network for connecting peripherals.

Do You Have Bluetooth?

○ **Windows 8.1 and later**: Hover over the bottom-left corner, right-click over the Start button and select Device Manager. Once in Device Manager, look for Bluetooth, with its characteristic blue badge and icon, in the list.

○ **Windows 7**: Open the Control Panel and select Hardware and Sound, followed by Devices and Printers.

Above: Accessing Device Manager.

HOW TO SET UP BLUETOOTH

It is easy to set up Bluetooth; just follow these steps:

1. Make sure that Bluetooth is turned on on both devices you want to connect.

2. On the PC, do this by pressing the Windows key + I to open Windows Settings (*see* page 50), select Devices, go to Bluetooth and slide the switch to on.

Left: Turn on Bluetooth on the PC by opening the Settings charm.

3. Check that the device you want to connect to is discoverable – or visible – so that you can pick up its signal.

4. Give your device a name to help identify it among the other Bluetooth-enabled gizmos (with some devices, Windows will do this automatically).

5. On the PC, scan for Bluetooth devices.

Step 5: Scan for Bluetooth devices on the PC.

6. Choose the device with which you want to pair your PC – in this example (see screen shots to right) it's a wireless mouse.

7. You may have to confirm the connection by inputting a code that appears on the other device. Windows will then pair with your device.

Step 6: Choose the device to connect the PC with.

8. Once you've gone through this pairing process, the two devices will automatically reconnect next time.

Troubleshooting Your Bluetooth Connection

If the connection fails, then make the device discoverable again; the signal is only broadcast for a short time, so it may not have been detected.

Step 8: The devices will now connect automatically.

○ **Can Your PC be Found?** Make sure that your PC can be found: go to the notification area on the desktop and click the Bluetooth icon. Choose the Open Settings command and, when the window opens, make sure that there is a check mark beside the option Allow Bluetooth devices to find this PC. Click OK.

○ **Check the Distance:** Bluetooth is for short-range networks, typically 1–10 m (3–33 ft). If the two devices aren't connecting, try moving them closer.

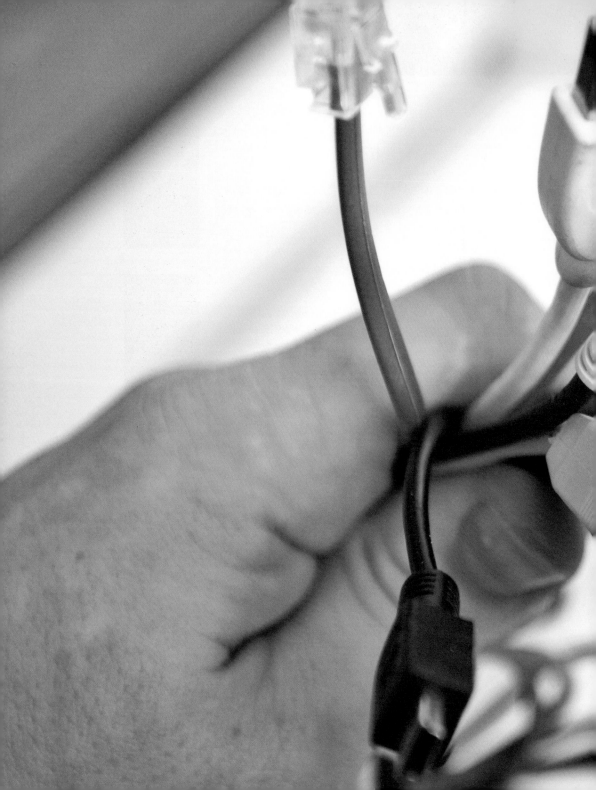

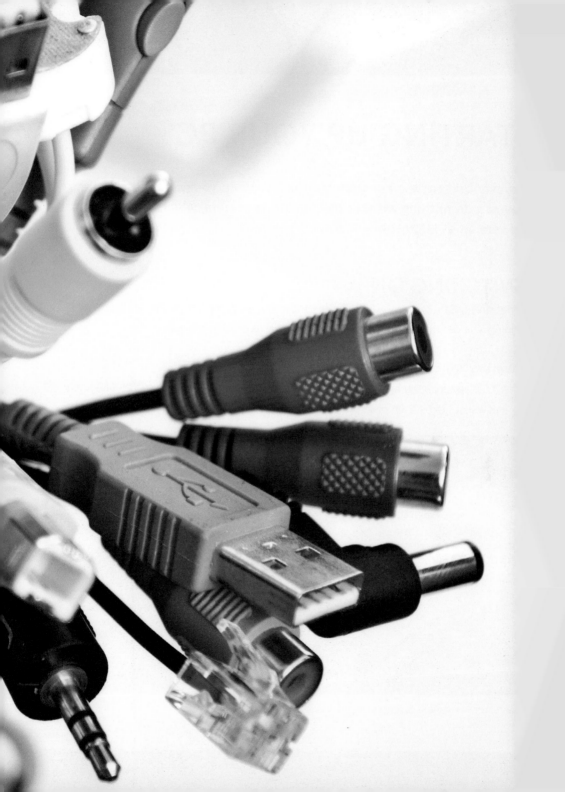

STARTING UP YOUR PC

However brilliant the components that make up your computer system, they can do nothing without the operating system, which for most PCs is a version of Microsoft Windows.

SWITCHING ON

It's not only the PC that consumes power – most of the peripherals do too. With a bit of planning, you can make the whole process as simple as flipping a switch.

Powering Your PC

Rather than attaching each of the different devices and PC units to a wall socket, plug them into a power strip that then plugs into the main power socket.

Above: The different tiles on the Start screen are part of the new Modern look of Windows.

It's best to use a power strip that has surge protection so that your electronic devices won't be affected by sudden spikes in the electrical flow that can burn them out. Don't plug a laser printer into a power strip – it draws too much energy and should be plugged directly into the wall socket.

Make sure that you have enough plug points in the power strip for all your devices. If you don't, buy a second power strip, but don't plug one into the other. Both strips have to be plugged directly into power sockets.

When you switch on the main socket, some of the peripherals will spring into life, as they have no separate power switch. Turn on any of the others before you switch on the system unit, so that the peripherals can initialize themselves and be recognized by the PC more quickly.

CHOOSING YOUR OPERATING SYSTEM

With current versions of Windows, you are getting two operating systems in one: the new Modern-look Start screen designed to look the same across PC, laptop and tablet, as well as the traditional desktop for organizing and working with your files. The main differences from the previous traditional Windows 7 look are:

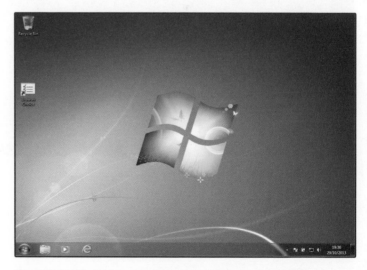

Above: Windows 7, which has a very different look, is based on the traditional desktop.

○ **Designed for touch**: Now you can close windows, access settings and select menu items flawlessly. Even if you don't have a touch screen, you can still operate Windows by gestures, using new touch mice and touchpad devices.

○ **Modern (Metro) look**: This is the new-look Start screen, featuring the same colourful live 'tiles' of information that were first introduced on Windows Phones. These are your Windows apps that you can move around, resize or remove. From here, you can also access the classic desktop that users of previous versions of Windows know and love. Originally, Windows 8.0 was without the familiar Start button for launching apps and accessing parts of the operating system. After much fuss, the Start button was reintroduced in Windows 8.1. Since this update users could start directly in Desktop view and bypass the Start screen completely.

Above: Many Windows apps, such as Maps, will show in full-screen.

○ **Windows apps**: Available in the Microsoft Store, both free and paid, they are specially designed for the Modern look. Most of these apps, like Maps, will show in full-screen.

○ **Action Center**: In one place you have all the system notifications and a number of settings, which give you quick access to adjust screen brightness, turn Wi-Fi on or off, enter Airplane mode and much more. To access it, click the icon on the far right of the taskbar and the Action Center appears in a slide-out pane.

- **Cloud services**: What you do on the PC is now closely linked with the cloud. For a start, you can save your files to OneDrive (Microsoft's cloud storage service) and then access them from any device. Microsoft also stores your settings in the cloud, so whenever you log on to a Windows device, using your Microsoft account, it will be set up the same way, just as you like it. Similarly, it allows you to share photos across several PCs.

- **Mobile-phone-style lock screen**: With a slideshow of your pictures, either from your PC or the cloud.

- **Snap views**: It lets you split the screen in order to have several apps on the screen at the same time.

Hot Tip

A number of apps come pre-loaded with Windows, including a calculator, voice recorder and Bing-powered health and fitness app.

Above: You can personalize the lock screen to cycle through your own pictures.

System Requirements for Windows

Surprisingly, as more features are added to Windows, the minimum requirements for running the operating system haven't changed. So, if you are running an earlier version like Windows 7 you can probably upgrade easily enough to the latest Windows.

- **Processor**: 1 gigahertz (GHz) or faster. It also needs certain extensions to handle memory and protect against attacks from malicious software. Windows checks during installation and, if you don't have them, will not install the new operating system.

- **RAM**: 1 GB for the 32-bit version, or 2 GB for the 64-bit version.

- **Hard disk space**: 16 GB (32-bit), or 32 GB (64-bit).

- **Graphics card**: Microsoft DirectX 9 graphics device or higher.

Remember that these are minimum requirements; in practice, you'll want both more power and space.

- **Using touch**: In order to use touch, you'll need a tablet or monitor that supports multi-touch. Using all the touch features of Windows requires at least a 5-touch-point screen.

- **Microsoft Store**: In order to access the Microsoft Store, you'll need a minimum screen resolution of 1024 x 768, plus internet connection.

- **Snap apps**: In order to snap apps, you must have a screen resolution of at least 1366 x 768.

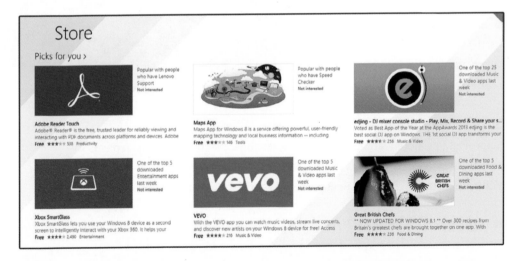

Above: A screen resolution of at least 1024 x 768 pixels and an internet connection are necessary for accessing the Microsoft Store.

Which Version of Windows?

When Windows 10 was launched, Microsoft declared it would be 'the last version of Windows'. That didn't mean no more Windows, simply that Windows 10 would become a Windows platform that would be continually updated without any jump in the version number. That's why,

throughout most of this book, we refer to Windows 10 as just Windows. For most users there are just two editions available (with 32-bit and 64-bit options available for both).

- **Windows 10 Home**: Primarily for consumers, you get all the benefits of the designed-for-touch operating system, with new-look Start screen and built-in apps, as well as the familiar desktop mode.

- **Windows 10 Pro**: Mainly for business use, or the tech enthusiast, this version has all the benefits of Windows 10 Home together with more advanced features, such as the ability to join a domain, encrypt your disk or log on to your computer remotely from any PC.

In addition, there are other editions of Windows 10, which are not generally available, that are designed for use in large organizations and education.

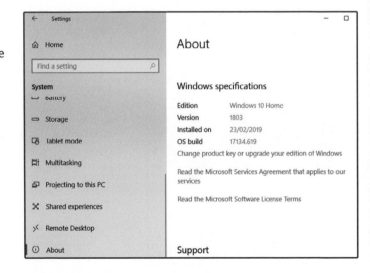

Above: By choosing System from Settings, you can find out which version of Windows you have on your PC.

Upgrade Routes

If you currently have Windows 7 Starter, Home Basic, Home Premium edition or Windows 8.1, you can upgrade to Windows 10 Home. If you have Windows 7 Professional, Windows 7 Ultimate or Windows 8.1 Pro, you can only upgrade to Windows 10 Pro.

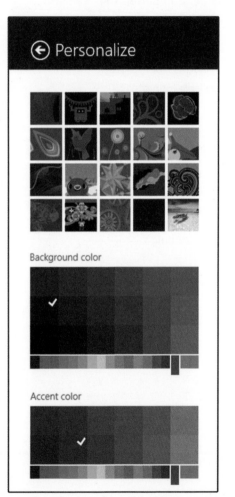

Background color

Accent color

SETTING UP WINDOWS

With each new version of Windows, installation has got simpler, so whether you're upgrading from a previous release or moving to a new machine, it is a painless process. Outside of some auction sites and stores selling old stock, it's very difficult to get a PC with Windows 7 or 8.1. And why miss out on all the benefits of Windows 10?

Installing Windows 10

1. When you switch on a new PC or laptop, it runs through a few initial tasks to set up the machine and get it working before you get to the first Windows 10 screen called Personalize.

2. If you bought Windows 10 online, double-click the file once it's downloaded, or load the installation USB stick if you have one.

3. When installation starts, you'll be asked to set your language preferences, enter your product key and accept the Microsoft Licence.

Left: After the PC runs through a few set-up tasks, the first screen you will encounter is the Personalize screen.

4. When asked, select Upgrade if you are moving from an earlier version of Windows, or Custom Install if it's a new installation.

5. If upgrading, make sure you have a backup of your files and settings, in case of problems with the installation.

6. During the installation process, the computer will restart itself – reboot – several times.

Personalizing Windows

Once installed, you can start to make Windows your own.

1. From the Personalize screen, select the main colour you want to use and type a name, without spaces, for your PC; finally, click next.

2. In the Settings screen, you can choose to let Windows set up automatic updates, personalize your apps and enable sharing automatically.

Hot Tip

If you are upgrading from Windows 7 or later, most of your apps should still work with Windows 10. But just in case, you should backup your data before upgrading.

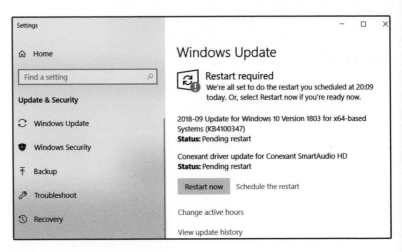

Above: Set Windows to update itself automatically and it will schedule a time to do it.

SETTING UP YOUR SIGN-IN

There are now two ways to sign into your PC: through a local user account, as before, or through a Microsoft account with your settings stored online.

Local Account

A local account is fine if you plan to work in the traditional desktop mode. With a local account, you can't run many of the Windows apps on the Start screen or get new apps from the Microsoft Store online. To set up a local account is simple:

1. When the Sign into Your PC screen appears, click Sign In without a Microsoft account and then select Local account.

2. Fill in the details with your preferred username and password, and add a password hint in case you forget it later. Click Finish and Windows stores your settings locally before playing an animation that shows how to use Windows.

Above: It is simple to set up a local account.

Microsoft Account

If you use the Microsoft account, all the Windows apps, such as People (contacts) and Calendar, will be available, with many more from the store. Your data and backups of your apps will be stored in OneDrive, Microsoft's cloud storage site.

Even if you choose not to use a Microsoft account initially, you will be prompted to sign up each time you access a Windows app. When installing Windows, you'll be asked to Add your Microsoft Account so that your settings can be stored in OneDrive.

Hot Tip

You can choose to get a new Microsoft email address when you sign up for a new account, which you can then use with the built-in mail app.

If you already use one of Microsoft's services, such as Hotmail, Live, Xbox Live, etc., you'll already have an account. Just enter your email address and password and it's done.

If you prefer, you can sign up for a new Microsoft account. Click the Sign up for a Microsoft account link and then enter the email address you want to use with your account and password.

Above: Upgrade to Premium OneDrive with Office 365 and you get 1 TB (1,000 GB) of online storage.

START SCREEN

In addition to showing off Windows' striking new look, the Start screen also accesses many of the PC's core functions, such as starting programs, changing settings and even shutting down.

METRO LOOK

The use of bold shapes, strong colours and solid typography, based on a design language that Microsoft originally called Metro, gives a common look to Windows PCs, tablets and phones.

Hot Tip

After a rumoured name dispute, Microsoft called the new look for Windows Modern, although most users still refer to it as Metro.

Above: The News and Sports tiles are live.

Smart Tiling

The Start screen is made up of a series of tiles, featuring different programs and apps which you can click – or tap – to open full-screen. Some of the tiles are live, i.e. they show the content inside; for example, the News tile pictures some of the latest headlines.

Navigate the Start Screen

Typically, all the app tiles won't show on screen. There are several ways to access the ones that are out of sight:

1. Use your mouse to scroll up and down the screen.

2. Move the scroll bar at the side of the screen.

3. On a touch screen, flick the tiles left or right.

4. Press the up or down, right or left arrow keys on the keyboard.

5. Press the Home key to go to the first tile, or the End key to jump to the last tile.

Launch the Start Screen

There's a lot of switching between full-screen apps, traditional desktop and the Start screen, but there are quick ways to do it:

1. Point to the lower-left corner of the screen and click the Windows (Start) button.

Above: Not all the app tiles will fit on one screen; you'll need to scroll left and right to view the rest.

2. Press the Windows key on the keyboard to switch between Metro and Desktop mode.

3. On some touch screens, you can press a Windows key on the casing just below the display.

Where to Start

In Windows 7 and earlier versions, a Start button on the desktop gave you access to your applications and various Windows functions. By popular demand, this has now returned – and so has direct access to the desktop.

Each time you start the PC, you will still have to log in through the mobile-phone-style Lock screen. The screen features a colourful background image, which you can customize, and the current date and time.

Click on the screen, or flick your finger up from the bottom of your touch screen, and you'll be prompted for your password.

Press Enter or click the right-pointing arrow and you're in.

ORGANIZING THE START SCREEN

The Start screen is the centre of the Modern-look Windows, where your online world mixes with your local workspace. The good news is that you can customize it so it's just the way you want.

Above: You can resize the Start screen to suit your taste.

Adding Tiles

When Windows 8 first launched, any new programs that were added were pinned to the Start screen. As a result, it got rather long. So now, in later versions of Windows, when you add a program, it joins a list of Apps on the Start screen. Access this by clicking or tapping the Windows button at the bottom of the screen, or by flicking the Start screen up.

It is simple to resize the Start screen to fit in more tiles. Move your cursor to the top corner of the Start screen until it becomes a double-sided arrow. You can increase or reduce the size of the screen but not remove it completely.

STEP-BY-STEP: ADDING AN APP TO THE START SCREEN

1. Choose the app you want to add to the Start screen. Here, it's the Evernote app for syncing and storing local files with their online service.

Step 1: Select the app from the app list that you want to add as a tile to the Start screen.

2. Right-click the app and you'll see a check mark appear in the top right-hand corner of the tile, plus the Option bar at the bottom of the screen.

3. Click Pin to Start and the tile will be added to the Start screen. If you prefer to work with the more traditional Windows view, add it to the desktop by selecting More, then Pin to taskbar.

Step 2: Right-click the app and various options appear.

4. The Start screen appears and you'll see that the tile for your app has been attached at the bottom. Right-click and you can resize.

Move Your Tiles

You don't need to keep tiles in their original position; you can arrange them any way you like. You could, for example, group together apps that you use for work, your

Step 4: Your chosen app will now appear as a tile on the Start screen.

favourites or all similar apps, such as music players, online music services and radio stations. In order to move a tile, just click it, drag it where you want and then release it.

Hot Tip

To see just the app tiles and remove the list of all applications from the Start screen, go to Settings. Choose Start and switch off Show app list in the Start menu.

Create a New Group of Tiles

In order to set up a new group, drag the tile you want to the gap between two existing groups. Once the grey bar appears, release the tile and you have the start of a new group. Now simply drag and drop the tiles that you want to add.

Above: To name a new group, type a name into the Name group text box.

Name the Group
Hover over the group until two white horizontal lines appear, then click, and write in your chosen name.

Expand Tile Groups
Would you rather see your groups of tiles extend across the full screen? It's possible to remove the background from the Start menu so that the pinned tiles are displayed across the screen. Press the Windows key + I to open the Windows Settings box. Select Personalization then Start. On the right-hand side turn on Use Start full-screen. At the top left-hand side of the screen you can choose to display just the pinned tiles or select the icon underneath to display All apps.

Hot Tip
Not all tiles have the same resize options. For example, the Mail app tile doesn't have a large option, while the Maps tile can only be Medium or Small.

Resize Your Tiles

Within the columns of tiles, you can change their size to help your favourites to stand out or to give more space to live tiles, such as Sport, which have constantly updating information. Right-click a tile or swipe down on a touch screen to select it and, from the Option bar that appears below, click or tap Resize. You can choose to make the tile Large, Wide, Medium or Small.

Remove a Tile

If your Start screen is too cluttered you can remove tiles you don't want: right-click the tile (swipe down on a touch screen) to select it and then tap or click Unpin from Start. This doesn't uninstall the app, which will still show in Search results – only the tile.

Above: To access the Action Center just click the icon at the right of the screen.

ACTION CENTER

Wherever you are in Windows, you can access the Action Center to help you manage notifications and carry out some of the regular things you do, such as connecting devices or changing settings.

Accessing the Action Center

The Action Center is always available to the right of the screen, no matter whether you are working with a Start screen or in full Desktop mode. Below are three different ways to access the Action Center:

○ Move the mouse to the bottom-right corner and click the square with the down-pointing arrow.

- Press the Windows + A keys on the keyboard.

- Swipe in from the right edge of the touch screen.

Search Box

The Search box lets you search within an app, within your files or across the web with the results appearing in one convenient place.

- **Search your PC and online**: Use the Filters at the top of the Search window to select which results you want to see. You can opt to search everywhere or filter the results to just show Settings, documents, folders or images and the like.

Above: The Search box allows you to search for items in a variety of ways.

- **Search within apps**: Open an app and there's usually a Search box within it. So inside the Mail app, you can search for a specific message, all emails from a particular person, and so on.

Sharing

Whether it's a document, photo or webpage, there are options for sharing content via email or social networks. For example, in Photos, right-click the image you want and select Share for the various options available. You can also share with a nearby computer. To do so make sure you both have Nearby Sharing turned on in the Action Center.

Start

It's quickest to open the Start screen using the Windows button, if you have one, or the Windows key on the keyboard. If you're on the Start screen, press the icon of the last app you used.

Devices

You can connect your app to the relevant device – whether it's a second monitor, printer or media player – open the Action Center and click the Connect button. Follow the on-screen instructions to link-up with the new device.

Settings

This is designed to help you personalize your PC, such as changing the background image on the Lock screen, as well as giving you quick access to a range of PC settings.

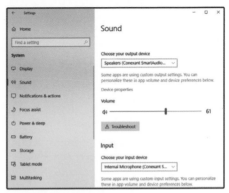

Network & Internet: Connect to the internet through the appropriate wireless or wired network.

Volume: Under System then Sound, the loudness level is shown by a number out of 100. Click on the speaker and use the slider to adjust the volume.

Display: Click System then Display and use the slider control to adjust the screen's brightness. You can also check the box to adjust the brightness automatically when lighting changes.

Notifications & actions: The messages that appear momentarily on screen to let you know that something has happened. For example, Mail will send a notification when a new email appears. Click System, then Notifications & actions to select which apps send notifications and where they appear.

Power & sleep: Listed under System settings, these options enable you to save energy and battery life.

Time & Language: Select Region & language to choose the language and keyboard layout.

Above: Windows Settings offers quick access to all parts of your PC.

Switching Off Your PC

The quickest way to shut down is to press the Windows key + X to open the power user menu and select Shut down or sign out.

- **Sleep**: Saves your work in memory and to the hard drive, but switches to low power mode to save energy. When you come back, wake up the PC or laptop with a touch of the keyboard and it will be just as you left it.

Above: Select Shut down or sign out, and then choose from one of the four options.

- **Shut down**: Switches off the PC, but does so in an orderly fashion, saving your work and closing all the programs that are open.

- **Restart**: A good way of clearing problems, such as Windows freezing or apps crashing. Sometimes, when you install a program, you have to restart before it will work.

- **Hibernation**: Principally for laptops, as it saves open documents and programs on the hard disk and then turns off the computer to save power.

Hot Tip

If shutdown options like Sleep or Hibernate aren't available, you can activate them. Open the Control Panel, select Power Options and choose what the power buttons do. In the window that opens, click Change settings that are currently unavailable and check the box beside any that aren't showing.

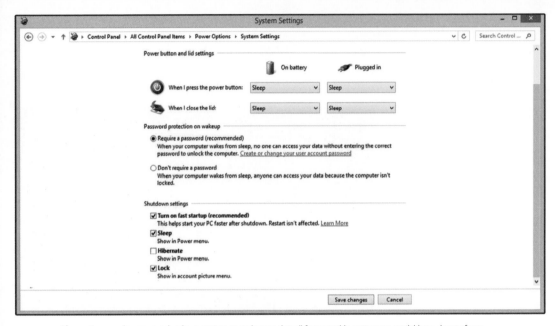

Above: You can change your shutdown settings to make sure that all four possible options are available to choose from.

PC SETTINGS

There are many more settings you can change from Windows Settings. To access them, simply press the Windows button + I.

Change PC Settings

○ **Personalization:** Lets you customize your PC, changing the Lock screen, background images, colours used and fonts, as well as the Start menu.

○ **Accounts:** Controls sign-in options and user accounts.

○ **OneDrive:** Sets which files and settings are synced with Microsoft's cloud storage service, so that they are available to you wherever you sign in with your chosen Microsoft account.

- **Apps**: Select the default apps for certain tasks, such as playing videos or browsing the web.

- **Privacy**: Decide how much personal information you will allow apps to access, as well as choose which ones can use devices on your PC, such as the webcam or microphone.

- **Phone**: Allows you to link your Android or iPhone to your PC, so you can start using an app on one device and then continue working with it on the other.

- **Cortana**: Select how your personal digital assistant will respond to your voice and where Cortana can be accessed.

- **Ease of Access**: For those who need help with using the PC, such as hearing what's on screen, magnifying text or different pointer colours.

- **Update & Security**: Where you can select which Windows updates you want to install, and back up and recover your files in the event of any problems.

Right: There are several PC settings which can be altered to change how you talk to Cortana.

WINDOWS APPS

In Windows, the programs that let you do anything – from playing music to organizing photos – have been renamed 'apps'. There are several built-in ones and thousands more available in the Microsoft Store.

WORKING WITH APPS

Windows apps are just like those you get on your mobile phone or tablet. However, you need to be signed in to your Microsoft account and online to access some of them.

Access the Apps

Windows' Start screen shows all the apps on your PC, including some of the free apps that come with the operating system. Some of the main ones are detailed here.

Above: You can schedule events in the Calendar app.

Built-in Apps

- **Calculator:** Not just for ordinary calculations, it includes converters for currency, volume, temperature and more.

- **Calendar:** Lets you schedule appointments and other events, or you can use it with existing online calendars, such as Google.

- **Camera:** Connects with a built-in webcam or attached camera to take photos or video.

○ **Groove Music:** Lets you listen to your favourite music on your PC or sounds that you've uploaded to OneDrive.

○ **Mail:** For sending and receiving messages through your Microsoft account or by linking up to online email accounts, such as Outlook or Gmail.

BING FINANCE

Merlin targets £3bn flotation

PRESS ASSOCIATION

Sainsbury's vs Tesco dispute winds up in court
The Independent

Consumer confidence on the increase
Press Association

FTSE 100 6,790.27   +15.54 ▲
FTSE Mid 250 15,559.61 +24.10 ▲
FTSE AIM All 808.18   +2.85 ▲

Above: The Money app is frequently updated with the latest information.

○ **Maps:** PC version of Microsoft Maps, which not only show locations but also give directions on how to get there.

○ **Microsoft Edge:** This is the default web browser for Windows. As well as being a browser you can use it to view PDF (Portable Document Format) files, such as your PC's manual or many email attachments.

○ **Microsoft News:** Another live tile, it has the news of the day as covered by different news services that you can select.

○ **Money:** A live tile, as it is regularly updated with the latest financial news and stock market prices.

○ **OneDrive:** The app for sending files to the online storage service of the same name that's attached to your Microsoft account.

Hot Tip

The Groove Music app lets you listen to your favourite music on iOS and Android devices, as well as your PC.

○ **People**: As you connect different accounts, such as from Twitter or Facebook, this app will automatically enter your contacts and their details.

○ **Photos**: Lets you view the photos on your PC, as well as on various online accounts, such as Flickr, Facebook or OneDrive.

○ **Sports**: Follow your favourite team or get the latest sports news directly to your desktop.

○ **Store**: Where you can find, buy and update Windows apps.

○ **Translator**: The app uses artificial intelligence to translate text into 60 different languages, including such as Yucatec Maya. It is also integrated with Cortana for voice translation.

Above: The Translator app works with Cortana for voice translation.

○ **Video**: Part of the Photos app, you can create your own videos and edit them from start to finish.

○ **Weather**: A live tile that tells you the weather near you or around you and forecasts for the days ahead.

Above: The Weather app provides the latest forecasts for a chosen location.

○ **Xbox**: Takes you through to Xbox Live, where you can play games from your PC or Xbox, and then go back and brag about your scores.

Starting Apps

In order to start an app, simply click (or tap if you have a touch screen) the program's tile.

Working with an App

Once the app is open, you can alter what it does by accessing its commands. For example, in Maps, you can drag and drop a pin to mark a location, change the style of map from road to aerial view, and more.

Hot Tip

An alternative way to open an app is to press Tab on the keyboard until the first tile on the Start screen is selected (it will have a white border round it). Use the arrow keys to select the tile you want and then press Enter to start.

In order to access this Options bar (also called App bar) with a mouse, right-click anywhere within the app and select the command you want. On a touch screen, swipe up from the bottom of the screen or down from the top.

Switching Apps

You can have several apps open at the same time, as they don't take up much system resource when not in use. This makes it easier to switch between apps.

- **Keyboard**: In previous versions of Windows, pressing the Alt key and Tab button (known as the Windows Flip) would open the list of running apps. By pressing Tab you could select the different apps. This still works. But now there's an alternative. Press the Windows key and Tab button to open the Task View. At the top, you can move between Desktops. Underneath you can switch between the open apps.

- **Touch**: Swipe from the left of the screen to open Task View. You can also tap (or click) the Task View button. If it's not showing, tap or right-click on the Taskbar and select Show Task View button from the menu.

Above: Task View allows you to move between desktops and apps.

Above: The mouse pointer will change to a hand when at the top of.the screen.

Close an App

There will be times when you want to shut down an app, such as when it's not working properly.

○ **Mouse:** Move the pointer to the top of the screen and, when it changes to a hand, click and drag the app to the very bottom of the screen, then release.

○ **Touch:** Drag the app from the top edge of the screen to the bottom.

○ **Keyboard:** Press Alt+ F4 keys.

Find New Apps

The ever-growing Microsoft Store is the place to find the apps to help you work, learn and play.

1. In order to see the full list of categories (plus Picks for you), the top paid and free apps, as well as new releases, right-click within the Store or swipe in from the right on touch screens.

2. Click or tap an app to see its details, including a description of its main features, price and any user ratings or reviews available.

INSTALL A NEW WINDOWS APP

Install a new Windows app by following these steps:

1. Go the Start screen and click Store app with its shopping bag icon. You'll need to be connected to the internet.

Step 1: Click the shopping bag icon on the Start screen.

2. Search or scroll through the different categories to find the app you want; here, it's Great British Chefs in Food & Dining.

3. Tap or click on the app and you'll see the details, plus the average star rating. The figure next to it is the number of people who have rated it. In order to read some of the reviews and get details about the app, scroll right.

Step 2: Scroll through the various categories until you find the app you want.

Step 3: Click on the app for further details about it.

Hot Tip

In order to make it easy for you to discover new apps you'd like, Store presents personalized Picks, based on your previous choices.

Step 4: For free apps, simply click Install.

Step 9: The newly installed app will now appear on the Start screen.

Step 10: Tap or click the app and it will open.

4. As this is a free app, you simply select Install.

5. For paid apps, tap or click Buy or Try (if it offers a free trial) and then confirm. You have to be signed in to your Microsoft account to install an app.

6. In the box that opens, you'll be asked to verify your account information and enter your password.

7. You'll then be asked to choose a payment method, which can be by credit card, from PayPal or directly from your Microsoft account, if you have funds in it. The amount available is shown.

8. When you have finished entering the details, click Submit.

9. In order to find the newly installed app, go to the Start screen, then click the downward-pointing arrow and the app will be there, labelled 'NEW'.

10. Tap or click the app to open.

Above: A message will appear when a new app is installed.

Install Your Apps on More Than One PC

1. Go to the Start screen on the PC which you want to install the apps and click Store.

2. Tap or click the More button (three dots) and select My Library.

3. Use the menu to choose whether you want to see all apps that you own. You can also see a list of which apps you have installed. Select Ready to install and you see a list of apps that you own, which are stored in the Microsoft Store cloud.

Above: You can choose to view only those apps not installed on this PC.

4. Click Show hidden products to show all the apps available.

5. Choose the apps you want to install and then tap or click Install.

Microsoft Store

← Home   Apps   Games   Devices   Films & TV

Settings

App updates

Update apps automatically
Off

Live Tile

Show products on tile
On

Above: It is possible to stop the PC from automatically updating apps.

Keep Apps Updated

Updates are usually free and can include improved or new features for your app. Now in Windows, apps are automatically updated in the background, so you don't have to do anything to get the latest features for an app.

1. In order to disable this (for example, if you are travelling), open Microsoft Store.

2. Click the More button (three dots) top-right and then select Settings.

3. Push the slider under Update apps automatically to Off.

You can still manually update your apps though:

1. Tap or click the Store tile and then the More button. Select Downloads and updates, then tap or click Get updates.

2. Choose which updates to add and then tap or click Install. You can carry on using your PC while the apps are being updated.

Uninstall Windows Apps

If your Start screen is getting very cluttered with apps you no longer use, you can remove them.

1. Go to the Start screen and select the app you want to uninstall by right-clicking or swiping down the app tile.

2. In the App bar at the bottom of the screen, click Uninstall.

3. A prompt box will ask you to confirm; click Uninstall again.

4. For more complex programs, you might be taken to the Uninstall or change a program section of the Control Panel. Select the program, then click Uninstall and, when the prompt box opens, click Uninstall again.

SCREEN SHARING

There are always times when you want to view different programs on screen at the same time, such as looking in the calendar to see if you're free for an event you're reading about on the web. Now you can, in a snap.

Snap the Apps

You can do more, faster, if you have several apps on screen together. For example, wouldn't it be more convenient to have access to your music player while reading a book? In order to do so, open both apps by going to the Start screen and clicking or tapping the relevant tile.

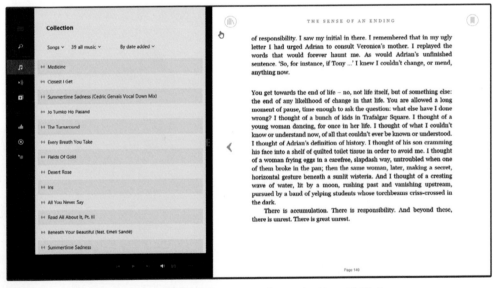

Above: It is possible to have more than one app open on screen at once; for example, a Music and a Kindle app.

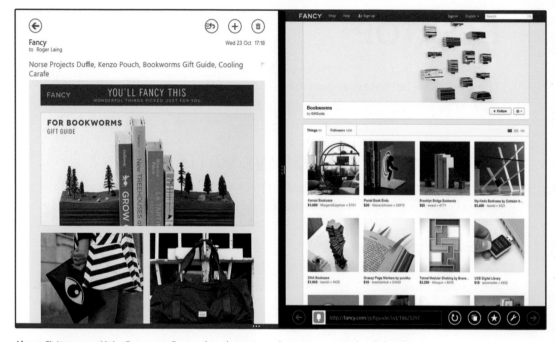

Above: Clicking an email link will automatically open the web page in your browser in a new window to the side.

1. Snap the first app in place by moving your mouse pointer to the top left-hand corner until you see the second app. Drag that app to the right of the screen until a purple space appears and drop it into place.

2. In between the two windows is a black bar with three dots and a white line in the middle. In order to resize the windows, click and drag this bar.

3. In order to unsnap an app, drag the bar to the left or right edge of the screen, or close each app (see page 74).

Hot Tip

Apps can automatically open another app beside them and arrange the windows side-by-side. For example, if you click a web link in your email it will load the web page in a new window next to your message.

DESKTOP

The desktop – an integral part of Windows from the start – is still the main area for working with your PC's files and folders.

TRADITIONAL WINDOWS WITH A TWIST

While the desktop with its Start button was the place to find and launch applications in earlier versions of Windows, now it can be switched with Tablet mode, which makes it more touch-friendly.

Accessing the Desktop

You'll know if you're in Tablet mode if the app tiles stretch right across the screen (with the desktop in the background). To revert to the desktop press the Windows key + D. If you prefer to use desktop mode by default every time you start Windows, you can set your PC to use Desktop mode rather than Tablet mode:

Above: If you'd rather work in Desktop mode, go to the Action Center and switch off Tablet mode.

1. Open the Action Center: press the icon on the far right of the Taskbar.

2. In the pane that slides out, locate the quick action button marked Tablet mode.

3. This toggles Tablet mode on or off. Switch it off to access the Desktop when you start your PC.

Guide to Desktop Features

While the main part of the desktop displays what's happening, the way your computer runs is largely controlled through the Taskbar. This is made up of the following:

- **Start button**: This has been in Windows since the start. It was left out in Windows 8.0 but reintroduced for later versions of Windows. Right-click and you will access the power user menu with many of the more useful tools needed to keep your PC running smoothly.

- **Pinned applications**: When you're running a program from the desktop, it appears in the taskbar. If you use the program frequently, you can pin it there to start it more easily.

- **Notification area**: Controls that alert you to what's happening with your PC and provide a quick route to change common settings, such as volume, date and time, and power options.

Personalize the Desktop

As with all versions of Windows, you can style the desktop your way, with your choice of background images, sounds and colours. Press and hold or right-click the desktop, then select Personalize from the menu that appears.

Above: Right-click the Start button and access the power user menu.

Above: Personalize the desktop to look and work the way you want.

NAVIGATING WINDOWS

Your PC is a mass of digital files that need to be organized to remain useful. Fortunately, Windows makes this easy.

Working with Files and Folders

All the individual items you work with, such as a photo or a report you've written, are stored as files. These are kept with others in folders on your PC's hard drive (or on your home network or the internet). Traditionally, Windows Explorer has let users manage files and folders, such as moving them to a different location or renaming them. While many of the functions remain the same, Windows Explorer has been given a makeover and renamed File Explorer.

Start File Explorer

1. In desktop mode, click or tap the File Explorer icon in the taskbar.
2. On the Start screen, type 'explorer' and select File Explorer from the search results.

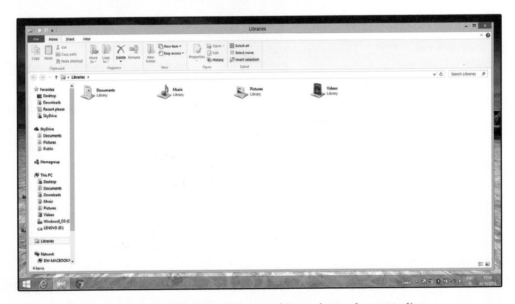

Above: Windows Explorer has been renamed File Explorer, but has many of the same functions for organizing files.

GET TO KNOW FILE EXPLORER

Navigation Pane

This lets you move between locations, such as your libraries, the drives on your PC or to other PCs on the network. In order to see those available, click the right-pointing arrow beside This PC.

Hot Tip

The background you choose for the desktop can also be used on the Lock screen for a more consistent look between Modern and traditional Windows. Right-click the Taskbar and select Taskbar settings. Select Lock screen and then in the Background section choose Picture.

Direction Buttons

○ **Back button**: Takes you to previous location or search results.

○ **Forward button**: Goes to the next location or search result.

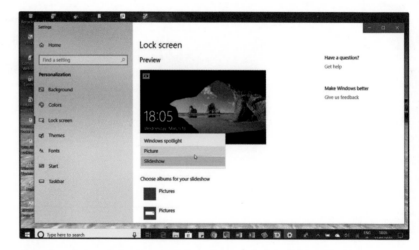

○ **Up button**: Opens the location of the folder that contains this folder (also known as the parent folder).

Above: For a consistent look, set the same background image for both the desktop and Lock screen.

Ribbons

The Ribbons include common tasks for managing, viewing and sharing files. Other ribbons appear according to the context. For example, the tabs are different if you select a folder in your Music library rather than your Documents library.

Reveal or hide the Ribbon bar by clicking the Expand the Ribbon button on the right-hand side of the menu, or by pressing Ctrl + F1 on the keyboard.

View Ribbon lets you customize the information that's displayed:

○ **Icon size**: Select from Small to Extra Large, depending on your preference.

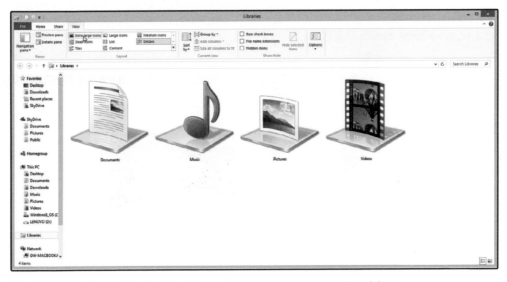

Above: View Ribbon allows you to customize how items are displayed; for example, icons can be made larger.

○ **List**: Alphabetical list of files and folders.

○ **Details**: Shows some of the properties of files and folders, such as the date and time they were last changed, and the size.

Hot Tip

Explorer includes the Ribbon bars that have become familiar in other Microsoft programs, such as Word or Excel.

- **Details pane**: Gives more information, such as the name of the person who created the file or folder.

- **Preview pane**: Lets you see the contents of a file without having to open it in an app.

Address Bar

Used to enter a location, it also shows the path to a file or folder. In order to return to a location you've visited recently, tap or click the drop-down list arrow on the right.

File List

It shows the contents of the current folder or library. There are four libraries, each of which stores different types of file.

- **Documents**: Stores all files that don't fit into the specialist folders, such as Music or Video.

- **Music**: Stores all your audio files.

- **Pictures**: For all your digital images.

- **Videos**: For your home videos and blockbuster movies.

Search Box

This looks in the current folder for the word or phrase you've entered. Search starts as soon as you begin typing.

Navigating Files and Folders

1. In order to open a folder, double-click or double-tap it, unless it's in the Navigation pane on the left-hand side of File Explorer, where you just need a single click or tap.

2. Contents are displayed in the right-hand pane.

3. You can keep opening folders – double-clicking them – until you reach the file you want. As you do, you'll see the path to the file change in the Address bar.

4. There may be many folders (subfolders) within a folder, and folders can be many levels deep. Use the Back or Forward buttons to go up or down a folder level, or click a folder name shown in the file path in the Address bar to go directly there.

Hot Tip

The quickest way to duplicate a File Explorer window is to select it and press Ctrl + N on the keyboard.

Above: The path to the file in the Address bar will change every time you open a folder.

Creating and Deleting Files

Usually, you will create a file with the apps you use, e.g. the family budget you've set up in an Excel spreadsheet. Typically, apps will save their files, by default, to the most relevant folder, such as a Word file going in Documents or a movie going in Videos.

In order to delete a file or folder, select it, tap or click the Home tab and then tap or click Delete. Alternatively, right-click the file name and select Delete from the pop-up menu.

Above: Right-click the file and select Delete from the menu.

Copy and Move a File or Folder

1. Select the items you want to copy or move.

2. Go to the Home tab and tap or click Copy or Cut as required.

3. Go to the new location and tap or click Paste.

Above: Drag the file or folder from one window to another to move it to a new location.

4. Alternatively, to move a file, open two File Explorer windows, put them side-by-side and drag across the file or folder you want.

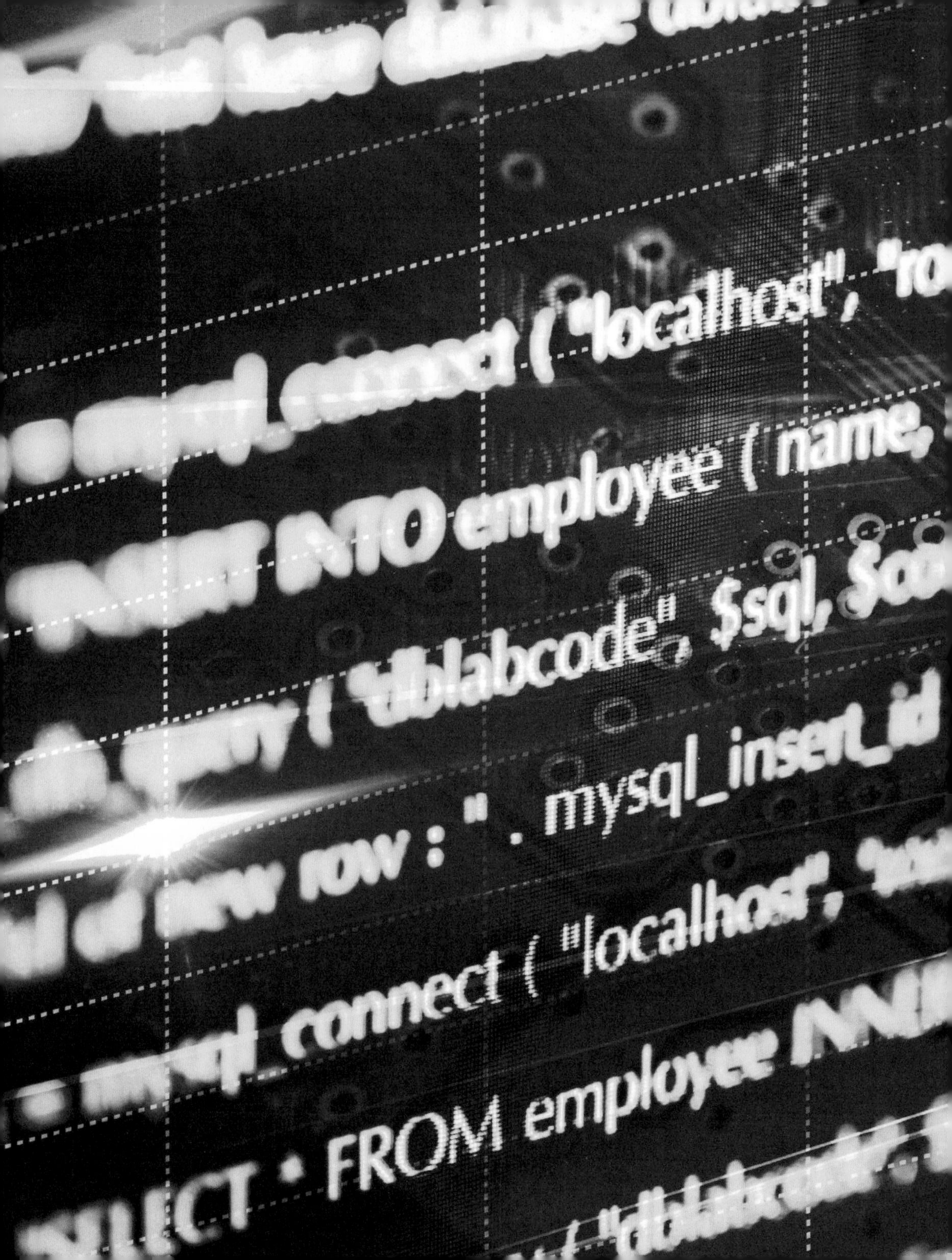
connect ("localhost",
INTO employee (name,
$sql,
row : " . mysql_insert_id
connect ("localhost",
FROM employee

PUTTING YOUR PC TO WORK

SOFTWARE

In order to put your PC to work, you need software: the programs that allow you to write, draw, record and edit video, play music, and so on.

FINDING PROGRAMS

If there's something you want to do on your computer, from designing your new home to creating paper planes, there's a program for it. And they're not difficult to track down.

What's the Right Name?

Software comes in a variety of guises and names:

○ **Operating system:** For example, Windows, which is the program that tells the computer what to do.

○ **Driver:** Software that operates (drives) specific hardware devices, such as the monitor or printer.

○ **Program:** Short for computer program, it's a general term that covers all software, from apps to games.

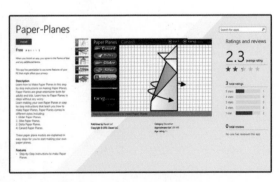

Above: You can find computer programs for just about anything – such as creating paper planes.

○ **App/Application:** Apps are generally thought of as smaller, mini applications, usually for smartphones or tablets. They are more limited in what they can do compared with applications. Applications are fully fledged programs, such as Microsoft Word or Adobe Photoshop, which enable you to be more productive and creative. However, Microsoft has done away with the distinction in Windows, where all programs are called apps.

INSTALLING SOFTWARE

Whether you get your program as a download from an online store or in the conventional way, neatly boxed-up and stored on an optical disc, you have to install it.

Installing Downloaded Software

With new-generation broadband speeds, it is relatively quick to download even large programs from internet stores. The process varies in detail but, generally, this is how to install downloaded software:

1. Once you have found the software you want, click the link to download or buy it. With paid software, the program will be added to your online shopping basket. You can either carry on shopping or click to go through to the checkout, fill in your details and buy your chosen program. If you are going for free software or trialware (where you have a limited time to try-before-you-buy), you'll start at the download page. In either case, there's usually a Download button or link to press to start the process.

Above: It is easy to buy and download software from the internet, much like buying other items online.

2. Depending on your web browser security settings, you might get a prompt box asking you to confirm the download. Typically, another prompt box asks whether you want to Open (Run) or Save the software. If you choose Save, you will have a copy of the software on your hard drive should you need to reinstall it later.

Hot Tip

Many download sites offer to send you, for a small charge, a backup DVD of the program in case you lose the downloaded file.

3. In the Save As dialogue box, you can name the program and select where to store it; by default, it will be your Downloads folder. Click Save and watch the Progress bar show the download being copied to your PC.

4. Once complete, click the Open button in the dialogue box.

5. It's likely that you'll see another security warning. Press Allow to start the installation and follow any on-screen instructions. These are specific to the individual programs, but may ask you to choose between different installation options or restart the PC to finish.

Left: Having completed the steps, the download will begin.

Installing Software from an Optical Disc

Once the usual way to install software, it has been overtaken by downloading for ease and convenience. Out-of-the-box software may have several discs, so look to see if one is labelled as the installation disc. Unlike downloads, it often comes with a quick-start or installation guide.

1. Insert the installation disc in the optical disc drive. Usually, the installation program runs automatically.

2. If not, you might see the AutoPlay dialogue box, asking you what you want to do with the disc. Choose Install or Setup.

3. Follow the on-screen instructions to complete installation and set up the new software.

> ## Hot Tip
> Even if a program doesn't add a shortcut during installation, it's simple to do so later. Right-click the program's icon and select Send to Desktop (Create Shortcut) from the pop-up list.

Easy-start Programs

Shortcuts make it easy to start your programs. During installation, most programs will ask if you want a shortcut added to the desktop; it is also easy to pin frequently used programs to the Taskbar at the bottom of the desktop. Here is how to do it:

1. Right-click the icon on the Start screen in Windows and select Pin to taskbar. This option is also available in Windows 7 if you right-click on a program's icon on the Start menu.

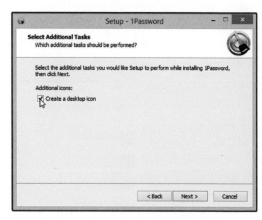

Above: Add shortcut icons to the desktop for easy access.

2. In Windows 7, you can also pin your favourite programs to the Start menu for quick access. Click on the Start button and then All Programs. Right-click the selected program and choose Pin to Start menu.

UNINSTALLING SOFTWARE

When you install a program, information about it is added to different parts of the operating system and deleting the program file itself won't remove these. In order to properly uninstall it, you have to let Windows do it.

Using Windows to Remove Programs

1. Go to the Control Panel.

   - In Windows, click the Start button in the lower-left corner, select Apps, then Apps & features.

   - In Windows 7, click the Start button, select Control Panel from the right side of the Start menu, then, under Programs, click on Uninstall a program.

2. All the software on your PC will be listed. Select the program you want to remove.

3. An Uninstall button appears; click this.

4. A prompt box might ask for an Administrator password. You'll also be asked to confirm you want to uninstall the program, along with any additional options available. For example, if deleting the web browser Google Chrome, you can choose to delete all your browsing data as well. Click the Uninstall button to finish the process.

Above: Select the program to be removed from the computer, then click the Uninstall button.

USING WINDOWS APPS

Thanks to its built-in, Modern-style apps, you can be productive from day one with the Windows operating system.

ORGANIZE YOUR LIFE WITH THE CALENDAR APP

The Calendar app will take information from your social network accounts, such as Facebook or Twitter, as well as Microsoft email accounts if you agree.

- **Information**: To see the information it has, click or tap the Calendar tile on the Start screen. It will open in Month view. If you want to change this, click the More button (three dots) and choose from Day, Week, Month or Year view.

- **Move back**: To move back through the calendar, click the left-facing arrow at the top, or press the right-facing arrow to move forward.

- **Add new appointment**: To add a new appointment, press the + button on the App bar and fill in the details of date, time and location.

1. If you have more than one email account set up, choose which associated calendar should show the appointment by selecting it from the drop-down list at the top.

2. Click the small disk icon in the right-hand corner to save the appointment.

3. If you need to change any details for an appointment, double-click the entry in the calendar.

Above: Keep track of appointments with the Calendar app.

MANAGE CONTACTS WITH THE PEOPLE APP

In order to get a head start in populating your contacts, you can link the People app to your social networks, such as Facebook and Twitter (*see* page 118).

1. For a more conventional way of entering a new contact, click the People tile on the Start screen, then right-click or tap an empty area to open the App bar and select the New Contact icon.

2. Fill in the details; you can access other headings, such as Job title or Website address and add notes by pressing Other info.

Hot Tip

If your contact is from one of the social networks you added, the delete button won't appear. You can only Delete these contacts by removing them from your social media account.

3. Under Account, choose which email account to associate the contact with, if you have more than one. This is particularly important if you want to sync contacts with your phone: for an Android phone, use a Google account, or your Microsoft account if you have a Windows phone.

People — □ ×

New Outlook contact

Name

Mobile phone

- ⊕ Website
- ▤ Company
- ✉ Job title
- ⚐ Office location
- ⚇ Significant other
- ⚇ Children
- ⚑ Birthday
- ♋ Anniversary
- ▭ Notes

4. Click the disk icon to save.

5. In order to delete a contact, click their name and, when their details appear, right-click an empty area to open the App bar. Click Delete to remove the contact or the pen icon to edit the details.

Above: Click + Other to enter more details about your contact, such as their birthday or job title.

GET DIRECTIONS WITH THE MAPS APP

It's easy to get directions using Windows' Maps app.

1. Select the Maps app on the Start screen.

2. When it first opens, a prompt screen asks Can Maps use your location? Click Allow or Block, according to your preference.

3. In order to search for a location, right-click in the app to open the App bar and select Search.

4. Enter the details in the Search box; it opens the map at that location. On the left-hand side, it shows the weather, drawn from the Weather app.

5. Having found where you need to be, you can then access directions for how to get there. If you have used Search to find the location, click the Directions icon by the pin on the map. Alternatively, select Directions from the Apps bar.

Step 1: Find the Maps app on the Start screen and select it.

Step 2: Choose whether or not to allow the app to use your location.

Step 3: To search for a location, open the App bar and select Search.

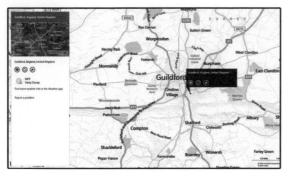

Step 4: When the map of the requested location is opened, the weather for that location will also be displayed.

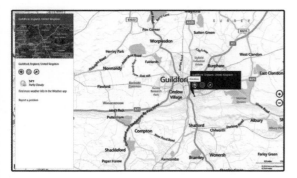

Step 5: Click the Directions icon on the map pin to find out how to get there.

6. Enter details of where you're starting in box A and the end location in box B. Click the Car icon if you are driving. Under Options, you can select whether to Avoid motorways or toll roads. If you are walking, select the Pedestrian icon.

7. In order to reverse the route, click the arrow beside box A. If you want to get directions, click or tap the arrow beside box B.

8. In the Directions window on the left, you'll see the first Route listed, with the distance and the approximate time it will take. Click or tap Routes to see alternatives.

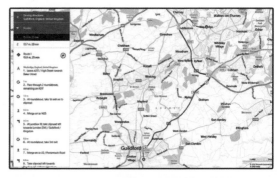

Step 6: Box A is the start location; box B is the destination.

Step 8: Alternative routes from the first route suggested are also available.

CREATE YOUR PERSONAL NEWS CHANNEL WITH THE NEWS APP

No need to miss out on what's happening around the world. The News app lets you see the latest articles in world news, technology, entertainment, politics, sports and more.

1. In order to open the News app, click or tap its tile on the Start screen. It opens on the Top Story, as selected by the editors at Bing. At the bottom, you'll see a small progress bar that says Downloading articles. Once finished, it gives the time of the last update and lets you know that the articles are ready for offline reading.

2. In the Get Started section, select Customize your news. Drag and drop tiles showing the different categories to rearrange the order in which stories appear. Click the X icon to remove them altogether.

3. If you want to add more categories, click the + sign and you'll see a list of possible categories on the left. Click on the desired one. You'll also see a list of publications with a brief description. For example, select Technology and you can choose CNET.com, The Register and *Wired* among others. Click the + sign to add that source to your news channel.

4. Alternatively, you can enter a topic to track or a source you want to use by entering their name or title in the Search box. For example, type Nobel prize and select the one you want from the search results by clicking or tapping the + sign.

Above: It's easy to keep up to date with the latest news around the world with the News app.

BETTER SURFING

When it comes to viewing websites, the experience can be helped or hindered by your choice of browser – and how you set it up.

CHOOSE YOUR BROWSING STYLE

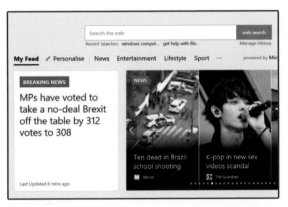

Above: Microsoft Edge opens with a newsfeed of stories you can personalize.

Above: Hover over a tab and you see a preview of the page.

Windows' default browser is now Microsoft Edge. But if, like many, you are familiar with Internet Explorer, the previous built-in browser, it is still available to download and run.

Microsoft Edge

Fast and simple to use, it doubles as a PDF reader.

1. The default Home page shows a newsfeed of the day's big stories. Enter a URL in the address page and the site opens in a new tab.

2. You can pin a tab so it's there for easy access. Simply right-click the site's tab and choose Pin.

3. As you hover over the tab you'll see a thumbnail preview of the site.

4. Click the Set these tabs aside icon at the top left. It sends the currently open tabs to the background.

5. Click the icon in the far-left of the button to restore these tabs when you want them. The set aside tabs are still available even after you shut down and restart Edge.

6. Edge can read any webpage aloud. Just right-click anywhere on a page and choose Read aloud. There's a choice of voices and you can pause and skip forwards and backwards through the page.

Above: Set aside tabs to read them later.

7. The browser also lets you read PDFs or ebooks, which you can buy from the Microsoft Store. Add these to your Reading list.

Hot Tip

Reading view in Internet Explorer removes distractions, such as ads, to let you focus on just the text on a web page. Go to the page you want and, if it supports Reading view, a book icon appears in the address bar. Press this.

8. You can access your Reading list by clicking the Hub icon and selecting it from the list on the left.

Choose Your Default Browser

In some regions, you will be asked which browser you want to run as default when you first install Windows. If you choose not to run the Microsoft browser, then Internet Explorer will only open in desktop mode in the future. If you plan to stay with Internet Explorer, which works with most current versions of Windows, then it is optimized for touch, so it's easier to tap in URLs, etc.

SPREAD THE MESSAGE

Remember the days before email? Or when chat wasn't something you could do online? It's hard to think now that digital messaging has become a vital part of everyday life.

EMAIL

Windows now comes with its own email program, so sending and receiving emails gets the full Modern look.

Setting up Mail

1. In order to add your email accounts, go to the Start screen and click or tap on the Mail app tile.

Above: There are various types of email account available to choose from.

2. Once open, select Accounts and then click the + Add account in the pane that slides across.

3. Now you can see a list of the types of account you can add, such as Gmail, Outlook or Exchange.

4. Once you've filled in your email details, such as username and password, Mail will configure the rest of the settings, e.g. outgoing and incoming server names. If it doesn't, your Internet Service Provider (ISP) can give you the details or they are often available on your ISP's web pages.

Hot Tip

If you use an Outlook.com email address as your login for your Microsoft account, Windows will automatically set up Mail to use that account.

MESSAGING

In Windows 8.0, there was a Messaging app, which you could link with your Facebook account to chat with your friends. That has now been replaced with Skype, which lets you make an audio or video call or chat, through instant messaging, all in one app. Skype's app automatically snaps to the side of a video you're watching or game you're playing so you can chat about it with friends.

○ **Earlier version?** If you have an earlier version of Windows, you can download a version of Skype for the desktop by clicking the Downloads link on **www.skype.com**.

Above: Skype is an excellent way to keep in touch, as it allows you to make a video or audio call or chat

PHOTOS

As practically all photos are digital today, i.e. stored in electronic format, they are a natural ally with the PC, which can be used to display, improve or alter them.

GET THE PICTURE

In order to use your PC's photo tools, you need to transfer the images to the computer, which can happen in several ways.

Transfer from a Digital Camera

You can transfer images directly from your camera to the desktop, as in previous versions of Windows, or in Modern mode, use the Windows Photos app. Firstly, you need to connect the camera, typically by USB cable. If this is the first time, you will see a notification in the top-right corner of the screen; tap to choose what happens to this device. When you tap or click the notice, there are several options:

Above: The Photos app imports all or a selection of photos to the Pictures library.

- **Import Photos and Videos:** Uses the Photos app to do just that. It can automatically import all the files into a folder labelled with the current date in your Pictures library. Alternatively, select which images you don't want to import and Photos will transfer those remaining. Once finished, click or tap the Open Album button to see your photos.

- **Open Device to View Files**: Takes the desktop route. It loads a memory card-style icon. Double-click to see your images in a folder on the desktop from where you can drag and drop them to the location you want.

- **Take No Action**: Cancels the importing of the photos.

Transfer from a Memory Card

This follows a very similar process to importing images from the camera. Windows asks what you want to do with removable drives (memory cards), and the options include using a Windows app to display the photos or opening them in File Explorer on the desktop.

Above: Windows will offer options for what to do with an inserted memory card.

Download Photos

In Windows 8.0, the Photos app could import photos directly from online services, such as Flickr, OneDrive or even Facebook. Although that feature has been removed, there are individual apps to access these services and, as with earlier versions of Windows, you can always use your web browser and download images that way.

Use the PC's Camera

Most laptops and even desktop monitors have a built-in camera or webcam. Although primarily useful for chat, they are also great for self-portraits. If you're running an earlier version of Windows, you should have software supplied by the manufacturer, whereas in later versions, you have the Camera app.

Hot Tip

Internet Explorer lets you download photos from websites and save them directly to your Pictures library. Tap and hold the photo until the App bar appears, then select Save picture.

Viewing Photos

Your PC will have several programs capable of viewing photos. This is how to use them:

1. The first time you open a new photo file type, such as a JPEG, GIF, etc., Windows may ask which one you want to use as the default. Choose the one you want from a list of the available apps.

2. Click or tap the first photo you want to view. If you've chosen the Photos app to display images, it will open full-screen.

3. Right-click and the App
    bar appears. Select Set
    as to send the picture to
    your Lock screen or
    create a photo tile for
    the Start screen.

Changing Default Photo App

You can change the default
program for opening a particular
file type. In the Photos app,
right-click to open the App
bar, select Open with and
make your choice. The traditional
way, from the desktop, is to
select Control Panel (by typing
the name in the Search box
on the taskbar or selecting it
from the Start menu in Windows
7), then View by Large icons
or Small icons and choose
default Programs.

Above: PCs are equipped with several programs capable of viewing photos.

Above: Set your preferred program as the default for viewing photos.

Hot Tip

At the top of the Photos App bar are the editing tools. As well as controls to
change the size and shape of an image, there are more advanced tools for adding
special effects and fixing basic problems like red-eye.

MUSIC

Whether you access music streaming services through a Windows app or via the web, you can listen to music collections with millions of songs.

IN TUNE

Apps like Spotify not only let you stream songs by your favourite artists, but also provide several ways to organize your music and access new tracks.

Spotify App

○ **Your Library:** Includes both music that Spotify has found on the PC and the playlists that you have added online to Spotify. This could be music you have purchased. On the left-hand menu you'll see that Your Library is divided into collections of your favourite songs, recently played, albums and artists as well as suggested tracks.

○ **Radio:** Lets you create your own 'station'. Click the Create new station link and then enter an artist you like. From that, Spotify creates a playlist of similar music.

Left: Radio can create playlists suited to your tastes.

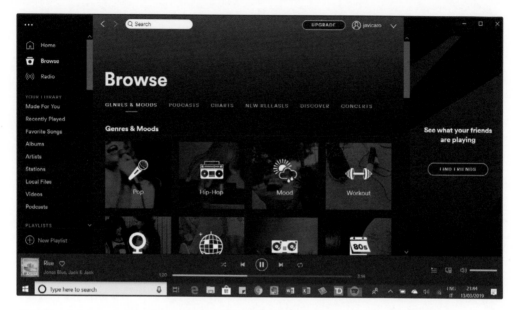

Above: Browse allows you to explore the music on Spotify by genres and moods as well as charts, new releases and more.

- **Browse:** Lets you discover music on Spotify. You can explore by artists, new and top-rated albums, and different genres. You can also select music that matches your mood – such as music for Monday motivation. Click the Play button to access the playlist and play the track. Right-click the More button and you can add to your playlist or Favorite Songs or share.

- **Playlists:** In the lower section of the Navigation bar. Now playing shows the current playlist with the playback controls at the bottom of the screen. Click or tap the + sign to create a new playlist, write a name and press the Save button. Click the Playlist name and

Hot Tip

You can also add tracks you like from your Radio stations to your playlists by selecting Now playing, the track and clicking the + sign.

you have the option to browse Spotify to add some music. If there's a track you want to add, select it and then click the + sign. In the pop-up list select, which playlist you want to attach it to, or create a New playlist.

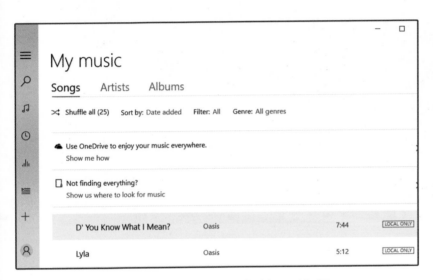

My music

Songs   Artists   Albums

⤨ Shuffle all (25)   Sort by: Date added   Filter: All   Genre: All genres

☁ Use OneDrive to enjoy your music everywhere.
  Show me how

☐ Not finding everything?
  Show us where to look for music

| D' You Know What I Mean? | Oasis | 7:44 | LOCAL ONLY |
| Lyla | Oasis | 5:12 | LOCAL ONLY |

Above: Groove Music can help locate your music on local drives and OneDrive.

Cloud Music

While Spotify will play back music it finds stored in your local files, that doesn't include any tracks stored on Microsoft's cloud service OneDrive. As you can get up to 1 TB of storage space on OneDrive, it's a good place to store your music MP3s.

So, Windows has its own music player – Groove Music. This will collect any MP3s it finds on your PC and on OneDrive. If it's having trouble locating your music, you can point to where your music files are, in the section marked Show us where to look for music.

Free Music Streaming

This is not quite as free as it appears. With a free account, you can only stream music to your PC or app. It means you have to be connected to the internet and the track is not stored on your PC. Your listening will also be interrupted by ads. With a paid subscription, you get unlimited streaming and can download up to 10,000 songs on up to five different devices, for offline listening.

Alternative Music Services

- **Apple iTunes (www.itunes.com):**
  Download the software which runs on the desktop and you not only have access to streaming music but can also purchase songs, albums and videos. You can also use it to sync your Apple iPhone, iPad or iPod.

- **Amazon MP3 (www.amazon.com):**
  A music store, but with the paid-for Amazon Cloud Player service, you can import your music collection, mix with your purchased songs and store them in the cloud. From there, stream the songs to your mobile devices and PC (using the new Amazon Cloud Player for the PC) or download them to play offline.

Hot Tip

Click or tap your profile icon in Spotify and you can see your most recently played artists with links to share the track on social media.

- **Google Play (play. google.com):** A paid-for All Access service which offers millions of tracks you can access via the web and from Android devices.

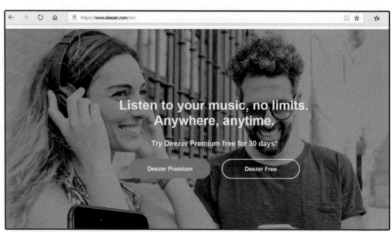

Above: Deezer.com offers over 53 million music tracks to stream.

- **Quobuz.com, Deezer.com and Tidal.com:** Online streaming music services. While the precise terms vary for each one, generally there's limited, ad-supported free streaming with different paid-for options, or a free trial period before you have to subscribe.

VIDEO AND TV

The PC is rapidly taking over from the television as an entertainment centre, with online stores making it easy to access the latest top movies and hit TV shows.

WORKING WITH VIDEO

In Windows you can not only buy and rent movies online, but also create and edit your personal videos stored on your PC.

Above: TV and film content is available to buy or rent from the Microsoft Store.

Finding the Blockbuster

Use the Microsoft Store app from the Start screen to go online and select Films & TV. Here, you can browse TV and film content that's available to buy or rent. The scale of it means that you have to scroll left or right through a series of screens.

- **New Films:** Scroll down the page and you'll see the pick of the latest releases displayed. To see more click or tap Show all. Keep scrolling to see top movie and TV rentals and more.

- **My Films & TV:** Shows any purchases made from the Microsoft Store, which can either be streamed to your PC (played live over the internet, so you need a good connection) or downloaded.

- **Top-selling Films & Top-selling TV Programmes**: You can filter these to show the best-sellers by ratings, sales, studio or genre.

- **Featured Collections**: These can be anything from James Bond movies to Zombie TV or Sales and specials.

Choosing Your Video

In order to see more details on any video, click its tile.

- **Movies**: Provides a description of the film, reviews from the film critics and a trailer. Press the appropriate button to Buy or Rent the film.

- **TV Shows**: Again, it gives a description of the programme. If it's a series, you can buy individual episodes. Click or tap the

Above: Clicking the title of a TV programme will open up more details about it.

one you want and select the Buy button from the pop-up box. If you know it's a good series, there's an option to Buy Season pass, which entitles you to stream or download every episode in that run.

Play Your Video

- **Play**: To start playing a video, simply tap its tile. It will begin playing full-screen with no controls visible.

- **Controls**: To access the controls, tap the screen or move the mouse.

○ **Pause**: Press the Play/Pause button to start or stop playback.

○ **Now Playing**: This shows how far you've gone in the current video, with a time stamp on the right. This circle, which is large to make it easier for touch control, is also the playback scrubber. Tap and move it left or right to go (scrub) back or forward through the video to the point you want.

○ **Movie information**: If available, this provides more information about the video.

○ **More Controls**: These are below the Playback bar. Among them is the Play to button, which lets you wirelessly stream selected videos to watch on a compatible device, such as an HD television.

Above: Press the play button to start playback.

Playing Other Video Content

There are many other sources of videos, most of which have their own video players.

Above: Vimeo is a website featuring uploaded videos on all sorts of imaginable topics.

- **Online stores:** e.g. Apple iTunes, Google Play, Netflix, Amazon Prime Video.

- **YouTube and Vimeo**: They feature everything from music videos to family disaster movies, such as Charlie bit my finger, where a baby bites his toddler brother's finger.

- **TV Players**: Several channels have their own dedicated player for watching their shows, most notably the BBC in the UK.

Hot Tip

Windows only plays items bought at the Microsoft Store. It won't play those from other online stores, as most are protected to prevent copying. This is the case in order to comply with the licensing arrangements with the major film studios and TV channels.

- **Earlier Version?** If you are running Windows 7 or earlier, there are a number of third-party video players available for watching movies, and the various video services can be reached via the web or their dedicated players.

GO CHAT

With social media becoming such a big part of everyday life, Windows makes it much easier to stay in touch with friends, family and colleagues by using Skype and other apps.

TALK WITH YOUR SOCIAL NETWORKS

The People app is an address book and social app in one. You can add your contacts and keep in touch with friends, family and your social contacts on Skype – all from the same app.

Add Accounts

1. When you first open the People app, you'll be prompted to add accounts. You can import contacts from apps such as Mail and Calendar, and Skype.

Step 2a: Get new apps from the Store at any time.

2. To add more accounts, click Apps and then Get more apps in the store. You'll see the available apps include Skype and some third-party contact manager apps as well as social networking sites, like Xing.

3. Once the app is installed, you'll need to connect the contacts in the new app to your People app. To do so, select Click to connect this app.

4. In this case, Skype wants to connect. A pop-up window asks you to confirm

that you'll Let Skype access your contacts? If you agree click the Yes button. You can always change this later by going to the Settings app.

5. Choose a profile picture, test your audio and webcam, if you have one, then continue. Now you're ready to start your own chat conversation or call using Skype.

6. To reach the people you talk to most, add them to your taskbar. Select People on the taskbar, then press the Find and pin contacts to see all your contacts.

7. Once you select a contact to pin they'll appear next to the People icon. Now you can message them directly from Skype. Click on their icon, then select Call with Skype from beside their phone number.

8. In the Skype box that opens you can choose to chat or call your contact or simply say hello by clicking the Wave emoji in the middle of the chat box.

Step 2b: Available apps include Skype and third-party social networks like Xing.

Step 3: You can connect contacts in Skype to your People app.

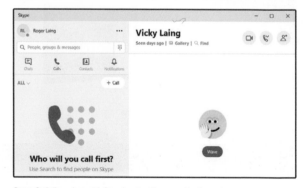

Step 8: Call or chat with friends using Skype or simply send a wave to say hello.

HOME OFFICE

Whether it's writing a letter, creating a school presentation, working out your finances or just managing your email, there are several software suites for running your personal office.

IN THE CLOUD OR NOT?

The best-known personal productivity suite, Microsoft Office, comes in several different flavours.

Office 2019 Suites

These are stand-alone versions of Office, which install the software on your PC. They offer different combinations of products. As well as the core programs Word (for creating documents), Excel (spreadsheets) and PowerPoint (presentations), there's Outlook for email, plus a mix of publishing and database programs.

Above: A subscription to Office 365 allows access to the latest Office applications, which can be used online or downloaded.

Office 365 (office. microsoft.com)

This is a cloud (online) service with a twist. With a paid subscription you have access to all the latest Office applications, with which you can work online, using web apps, or download versions of the programs to your PC to use off-line.

- **Multiple users**: It's good for families, as the download versions can be used on up to five PCs and five mobile devices, such as tablets.

- **Go online**: You need to go online each time you want to install Office on a machine and also to check for any software updates.

- **Syncing**: Documents and such that you create can be stored in OneDrive and synced with your PCs and mobiles, so they are safe and you always have the up-to-date version.

Office Workers

There are other office suites for working with text, spreadsheets and the like:

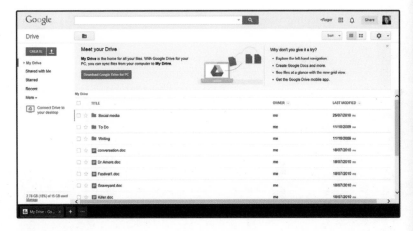

Above: Files can be uploaded, worked on or created in Google Drive.

- **Google Drive**: Offers a cloud-based service with up to 15 GB of free storage and the option to upgrade for more features. You can upload the files that are important to you and use the built-in web apps to create and work on new documents, spreadsheets and presentations.

- **OpenOffice**: A stand-alone productivity suite, like its rival Office, but only works offline. There is not currently a cloud version for syncing files, but it is free and can be installed on as many PCs as you like.

Hot Tip

Using Google's browser, Chrome, you can work on your Drive files offline; otherwise, you will have to work via the internet.

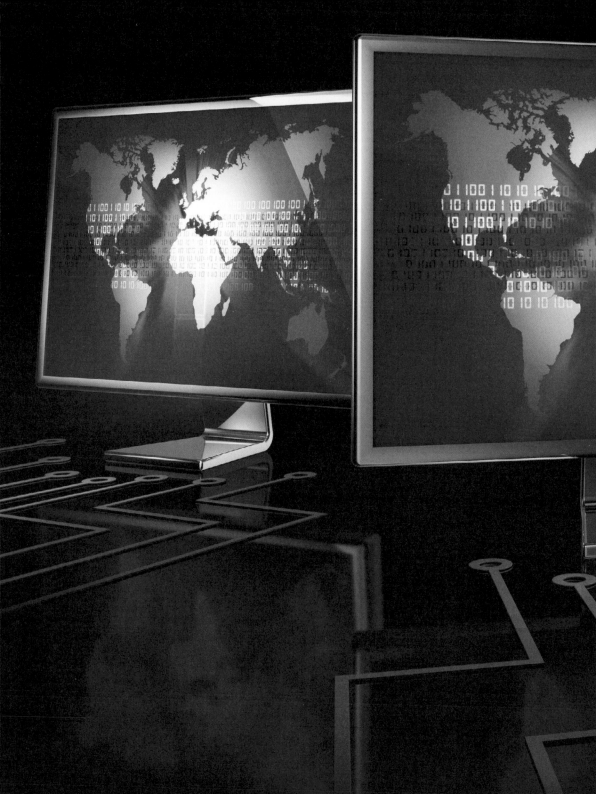

NETWORKS

HOME NETWORK

Once rare, it's now almost essential to have a home network to let different family members share files across PCs, play games and access the printer and internet connection.

SETTING UP YOUR NETWORK

There's a confusing amount of terminology around networking, which you need to understand in order to set up your network properly.

Types of Network

These days, most PCs are part of a network. In essence, a network is two or more PCs and assorted equipment, such as printers, linked together. You may see them referred to by different names according to the location of the networked computers.

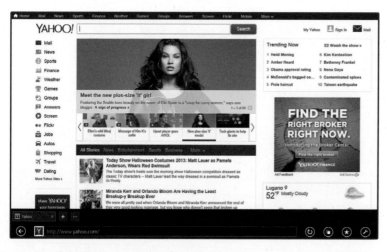

Above: The internet is the biggest network of them all.

○ **Home area network (HAN):** Most likely what you want, where all your digital devices within the home are connected.

○ **Local area network (LAN):** Similar, this describes home or office networks where the computers are close together, in the same building or house.

- **Wide area network (WAN):** Such as the internet, this is where computers are geographically far apart and connect over phone lines, cable or satellite and such.

WHAT YOU NEED

Make sure that you have all the hardware necessary to set up your wired network.

A Network Adapter

For PC or laptop, also known as network interface cards (NICs) or network cards. Most desktop PCs have a built-in network card with an Ethernet port, into which you plug the network cable.

Hot Tip
Although some laptops have Ethernet connectors, most new models come with a wireless network card, instead so that they can connect wirelessly.

A Router

This is a small box that connects PCs on your home network and co-ordinates all that's happening, as well as providing access to the internet. As it sits at the junction between these two different types of network, the router is also sometimes referred to as a gateway. With a router, several PCs can share the same internet connection. In addition, it may also act as a firewall, protecting your local network from intruders trying to access your computer from the internet.

The speed at which the router can move data around the network is important. The faster the better, although it can only work as fast as the other

NETGEAR

	LAN Speed Test	– ▢ ✕

Status

Ope

Writing

Cc Reading

Packet: 8 of 10   [Cancel]

Packet Size (Bytes): 1,000,000   **Packets:** 10

Folder or Server IP: \\DW-MACBOOKAIR\rogermacair\Public ⌄ [...]

	Writing (Upload)	**Reading (Download)**
Time / Packet:	0.5958141	0.4414567
Time to complete:	5.9581406	3.0901966
Bytes per second:	1,678,376	2,265,228
Bits per second:	13,427,008	18,121,824
Mbps (Default) ⌄	**13.4270080**	**18.1218240**

Throughput: ◉ Average ○ Maximum ○ Minimum   [Log] [Email]

Status: Reading Data...

Date:

[View Log File] [Clear Results] [Exit] [Start Test]

☐ Log Results   Version 3.4.0 © (2008-2012) Totusoft.com

Above: Network speed determines how quickly files move between computers.

Hot Tip

Network speed is how quickly you can move files between your computers and is important if you're backing up to an external hard drive. Internet speed, which is how fast a web page like Facebook loads, is different. It is much slower and governed by your broadband speeds.

bits of the network allow. So, if the network adapters on your PCs can't handle the data as quickly as the router, the latter can't work to its full potential.

Modem
Usually combined with the router, the modem sends and receives information over telephone lines or cable.

Ethernet Cable
To connect the PCs to the router. The cables have to meet certain standards, related to the speed at which they can transfer the data and also how well they prevent interference between the wires inside the cable. The highest at the moment is Category 7 cable, which supports 10-Gigabit speeds (10,000 Megabits per second) – that's fast.

Hubs and Switches
These are other terms you might come across. Hubs physically connect PCs and such into one network. Ethernet switches also connect all your network equipment. While the hub sends every bit of information round the entire network, the switch sends it directly to the PC or device that needs it. This is much quicker and puts less strain on your network.

Putting It All Together

1. Plug one end of the Ethernet cable into the network port on your PC and then the other end into a network – Ethernet – port on the router.

2. Every router has at least one network port. In addition, most routers have a built-in switch with extra Ethernet ports, so you can attach your PCs, hard drive, etc. directly. If you need extra ports to expand your network and add more devices, then buy a switch and plug it into one of the Ethernet ports on the router.

3. If your router only has one network port and you want to connect several devices, you'll have to plug them into a hub, or preferably a switch, and then plug that into the router.

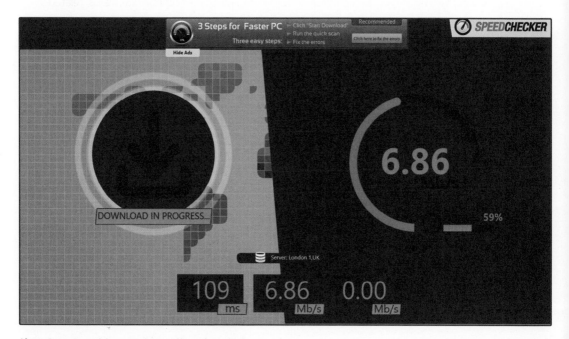

Above: Internet speed determines how quickly a webpage loads.

GETTING ONLINE: USING BROADBAND

In order to get the most from your digital life, you'll want to set up an internet connection that you can access from any of your networked PCs.

High-speed Internet

If you're planning to stream movies or music, play games online, or regularly back up large files to the cloud, you'll need one of the fastest broadband connections.

- **ISP**: The first step is to sign up with an Internet Service Provider (ISP). The price of your plan will vary according to the speed you want and usage, i.e. how much bandwidth you use a month by downloading and uploading data.

- **Going slowly**: If you exceed your limit, the ISP might slow down your connection (which may also happen at peak times when demand is heavy) or restrict what you can do.

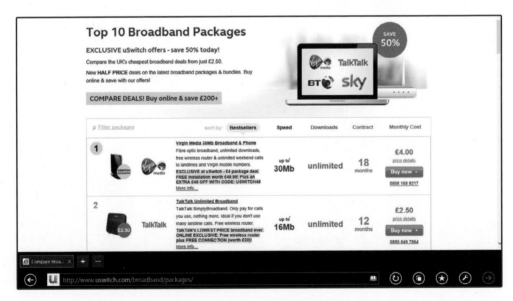

Above: A broadband comparison website will help you decide which option is best for you.

Broadband Options

There are many ways to get connected via broadband; here are the most common ones:

○ **ADSL broadband**: Over normal phone lines, with speeds up to 20 Megabits per second (Mbps). In order to prevent interference with your voice calls, a splitter – filter – may be added to your phone point, that has separate ports for the phone line and Ethernet cable.

○ **Fibre optic broadband**: More commonly known as cable, it comes in two flavours.

1. **Fibre-to-the-premises (FTTP) broadband**: Uses fibre all the way to your house and achieves the highest speeds, up to 330 Mbps. At that speed, ISPs claim you could download a music album in two seconds and an HD film in about two minutes.

Above: Both types of fibre optic broadband offer high speeds.

2. **Fibre-to-the-cabinet (FTTC) broadband**: Uses fibre all the way to your street and then runs over the normal copper telephone lines to your home. Advertised speeds are up to 72 Mbps.

> # Hot Tip
> ADSL stands for Asymmetric Digital Subscriber Line. It's asymmetric because download speeds are faster than upload speeds.

Setting up the Router

Whichever service you choose, your ISP will provide you with a compatible broadband modem, complete with instructions on how to set it up.

1. The modem is usually combined with a router in one device. In order to add it to your network, take the phone cord (or cable) and plug one end into the wall jack and the other into the port labelled 'wide area network' (WAN) on the router.

2. Take the Ethernet cable and plug one end into the port labelled 'local area network' (LAN) on the router (or switch if the network has been expanded) and the other end into the network port of the PC you want to connect to the internet.

Connecting with Windows

Usually, if you follow the ISP's instructions, you will already be connected to the internet. Launch your web browser and see if you can access a site you know.

Troubleshooting the Connection

If you can't connect, try these troubleshooting tips:

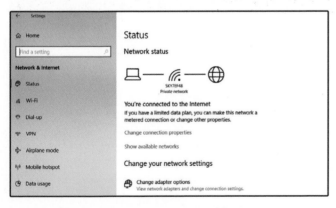

Above: Check the network connection through Windows Settings.

○ **Try the connection:** In Windows press the Windows key + I to open the Settings box (or click the Windows icon on-screen and select Settings from the Start screen). In Settings select the Network & Internet section. In Windows 7, click the Network icon in the notification area. Select the network you're trying to connect to and select Connect.

- **Set a new connection**: In Windows type Control Panel in the search bar at the bottom of the Desktop. In Windows 7, click the Start button and then Control Panel. In the Control Panel search box, type 'network', then select Network and Sharing Center. When it opens, click Set up a new connection or network and then double-click Connect to the Internet and follow the on-screen instructions.

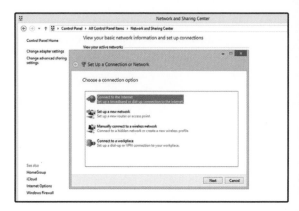

Above: Another troubleshooting option is to set up a new connection.

- **Start the network troubleshooter**:
  Open the Control Panel as before, select Search and enter the phrase 'Identify and repair' in the box. From the results obtained, select Identify and repair network problems. In Windows 7, click the Start button, select Control Panel, View by Large icons or Small icons and choose Troubleshooting.

NETWORKS WITHOUT STRINGS

Once only for the brave, wireless networks are now recommended over wired networks, as they give you much more freedom in relation to where you can use your PC. These networks are also known as WLAN, which stands for 'wireless local area network'.

Wireless Networking

Thinking of going wireless? Not exactly sure what this means? Read on!

- **Cable-free**: A wireless network is ideal for those who want to use their laptop around the house and to have several PCs share the same internet connection without the clutter of cables.

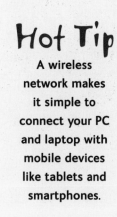

Hot Tip

A wireless network makes it simple to connect your PC and laptop with mobile devices like tablets and smartphones.

- **Radio waves**: Wireless connections use radio waves (radio frequency – RF – signals) to send information between PCs. These radio signals are like those used in commercial radio stations, but use a different frequency.

- **Transmitter**: For wireless to work, there needs to be a transmitter, which sends out the signals, and a receiver to pick them up.

- **A two-way thing**: Since, in networking, there is a two-way flow of information, most devices are radio transceivers, i.e. they can both send and receive radio signals.

Wireless Standards

When buying wireless equipment, you need to be aware of the standards they support: 802.11ax is the newest standard of Wi-Fi and, although it's compatible with older standards, it will only work as fast as the slowest part. Known as Wi-Fi 6, it's faster and about four times more efficient than the previous Wi-Fi 5 standard. It also operates at a frequency that's less prone to interference from other household devices, such as cordless phones or microwaves.

Wi-Fi 6 - The New Standard of WiFi

NEXT GENERATION AX WIFI

Above: Wi-Fi 6 is four times more efficient than its predecessor.

Setting up a Wireless Network

In order to set up your wireless network and connect to the internet, you'll need the right hardware:

- **Wireless network adapter**: Also known as wireless NIC or wireless network card. Almost certainly built into newer laptops, if you don't have one, you'll need an add-on adapter. On older laptops, there are models that go into the credit-card-size PCMCIA slot (PC Card). For more recent laptops and desktop PCs without a wireless adapter, there are USB versions.

- **Wireless router**: Has the same function as a standard router of connecting your local home network to the internet. In addition, it is a wireless access point (AP) that connects the wireless part of your network to the wired section.

- **Wireless antennaes**: Plug into most wireless equipment to boost the strength of the signal. Wireless repeaters, which connect to routers or access points, do the same and can also expand the signal range.

Above: Wireless routers are wireless access points as well as a standard router.

Connecting to Your Wireless Network

Most routers can now be set up wirelessly – and automatically – in Windows. Look for the Windows logo or the phrase Compatible with Windows on the router. This shows it uses Windows Connect Now.

CONNECTING TO THE INTERNET - WIRELESSLY

Here's how to connect wirelessly to the internet.

1. Press the Windows key + I to open Settings, then select the Network & Internet section. (In Windows 7, press the Network icon in the notification area). If it's marked Unavailable, it means that Wi-Fi is switched off.

Step 1: Select Network & Internet from Windows Settings.

2. Once the Networks page opens, go to Wi-Fi and slide the switch to On.

3. Once wireless is switched on, click Show available networks. They open the Action Center pane. Next to each name, you'll see there's a series of bars, which show the signal strength. If it's an unsecured connection, it will have a warning exclamation mark beside it.

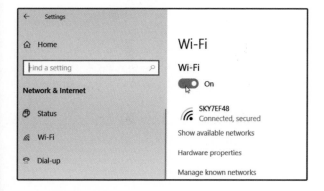

Step 2: Slide the Wi-Fi switch to On.

Step 3: You will see a list of available networks.

4. Select your wireless network name from the list.

5. If you check the box beside Connect automatically, Windows will set up that wireless connection every time you start your computer. Press Connect, and in the box that opens, enter your network security key, i.e. your password.

6. Tap or click Next and Windows will offer to set up sharing on the network and automatically connect your PC to devices it finds. This is recommended for home and office networks.

7. Click Yes if you agree, otherwise No, and Windows will connect you to your chosen wireless network.

8. If you change network, or don't want to be automatically logged in, follow the same process to select your network and click the Disconnect button.

Manual Setup

You can always connect manually to the internet if wireless is not for you.

1. Plug the router into a power source.

Step 5: Set the computer to Connect automatically to that network every time.

Step 8: Click the Disconnect button to change networks.

2. Get an Ethernet cable and connect one end to the PC's wired network card and the other into any LAN port on the router (avoid any ports labelled Internet, WAN or Uplink).

Above: To connect to the internet manually, set up the router as described.

3. On the PC, open your web browser and enter the setup page for the router. This will be in the ISP's instructions, but typically is http://192.168.0.1 or http://192.168.1.1.

4. Sign in with the username and password supplied with the router, then, in the Wi-Fi or wireless section, fill in the following details:

    ○ **Network name:** Also called service set identifier or SSID.

    ○ **Authentication:** More particularly, the type of encryption used for passwords and such to stop just anyone accessing your network.

    ○ **Security key:** The password that unlocks access to your network.

WIRELESS SECURITY

Wireless networks can be either open or secure. It is best if your home network is secure, in order to prevent strangers logging on to your network and accessing all your files or simply using your internet connection to get on the web.

A network is secured by encrypting the data. In order to get the key to the code used for encryption and connect to the network, you need the password, or security key. You can also safeguard access to your router by changing the default username and password supplied by the manufacturer.

Above: Password-protect your home network to keep it secure and prevent others using it without permission.

Hidden or Nameless Wireless Networks

Some people hide the name (SSID) of their wireless network in the belief that it will make it harder for any intruder to connect. That is debatable, but if you do want to connect to a nameless network, you'll have to do so manually.

1. Open the Network and Sharing Center in the Control Panel (*see* page 139). Click the link to Set up a new connection or network, select Manually connect to a wireless network and click Next.

2. Here, you'll fill in details of the wireless network. In particular, the network name (SSID), the type of security used, if any, and network password.

3. If it's your own network, you can get the details from the router (*see* page 139) on the page labelled Wi-Fi or wireless. If it's a friend's or work network, then you'll have to ask for the information.

4. As Windows can't detect a hidden network, check the boxes beside Start this connection automatically and Connect even if the network is not broadcasting, click Next and the network will be added.

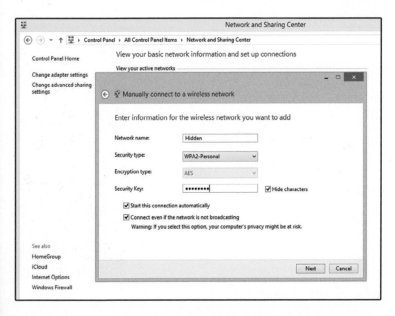

Left: You will have to connect manually to a hidden network by filling in all the details, such as name and password.

SHARING ON YOUR NETWORK

Wherever you are in the house, you can share files, media and even a printer using the home network – once you allow it.

CONTROLLING YOUR NETWORK

In order to make it easier to organize your home network, Windows has gathered together all the settings in one place: the Network and Sharing Center.

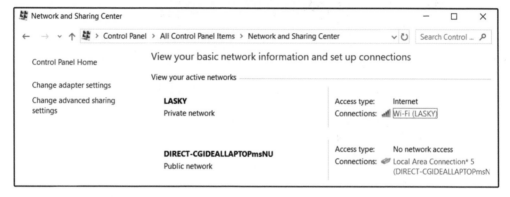

Above: Access the Network and Sharing Center from the Control Panel. From here, it's easy to organize your home network.

Network and Sharing Center

1. To access the Network and Sharing Center, go to the Control Panel (type in the Search bar in Windows, or select it from the Start menu in Windows 7), select Network & Internet, and click to open Network and Sharing Center.

2. At the top of the main section are details of your current active network. Underneath the network name is the network profile, which will be Private (Home in Windows 7) or Public, while on the right, you can see the access type (Internet, etc.), and the connections.

3. Among the networking settings are links to:

    ○ **Set up a new connection or network**: Such as broadband or dial-up, router or access point.

    ○ **Troubleshoot problems**: Lets you launch the network troubleshooter to attempt to diagnose the cause of problems and fix them.

4. In the left-hand panel are links to change adapter settings and sharing options.

5. Further down are links to controls for changing Internet Options and configuring Windows Firewall, which helps to protect your network from attack via the internet.

Above: There is a shortcut to accessing the Network & Internet settings. Right-click the network icon in desktop mode.

Hot Tip

There is a quick way to open the Network & Internet settings in desktop mode or in Windows 7. Right-click the network icon in the notification area and choose Open Network and Sharing Center from the pop-up window.

SETTING UP A HOMEGROUP

As part of Windows 7, 8.1 and earlier versions of Windows 10, HomeGroup simplifies sharing files and devices, such as printers, with every PC in the house.

Create a HomeGroup

Follow these steps to create a HomeGroup:

1. Each time a PC joins the network, a prompt box opens to ask if you want to find PCs, devices and content on this network. This is effectively turning on network sharing, so you need to say Yes in order to create a HomeGroup.

2. Open the Network and Sharing Center in the Control Panel from the desktop, or, in Windows 8.1, go to Settings in the Charms bar, select Change PC Settings and then Networks. In either case, click HomeGroup.

3. If a HomeGroup doesn't exist already, there will be a Create button. Press this.

4. Select which items you want to share with the HomeGroup by switching the sliders on.

5. As you turn on each share item, the screen dims and a message says You can keep using your PC while we apply these settings.

Step 3: Press the Create button.

Step 4: Switch on each item to be shared with the HomeGroup.

Step 6: The password generated by Windows has to be used by anyone joining the HomeGroup.

6. In the password section, you will see the random password generated by Windows, which will be needed for anyone else to join the HomeGroup.

7. If there's a Join now button when you go to HomeGroup it means that the network already exists.

Step 7: The Join now button means the network already exists.

8. Click Join now and follow the wizard to choose what you are happy for others to share and to verify the password.

Step 8: You can now choose which files can be shared.

HomeGroup Passwords

When a HomeGroup is created, either by Windows or a user, a random password is generated that has to be used by all who join.

1. You can see this password by going to HomeGroup in the Control Panel or PC settings.

2. In desktop mode, you may also be able to see it by going to File Explorer, right-clicking HomeGroup in the left pane, and selecting View the HomeGroup Password.

3. You can only change the password once you are part of a HomeGroup, and it has to be done through the Control Panel. In the HomeGroup window, click Change the password.

4. Confirm that you do want to make the change and Windows generates a new password. If you don't like it, you can use your own password by typing over the one suggested by Windows.

Above: You may wish to change the password to one of your own choosing.

Discover What's Shared

In order to see all that's available within your HomeGroup, head for the desktop and open File Explorer.

1. Click HomeGroup in the Navigation bar on the left and you'll see a list of all those who are sharing files.

2. Double-click any of the shared folders and libraries to look inside. By default, most of the content that is shared is read-only, so you can't change or delete it.

3. This can be changed using the Share tab in File Explorer. Select a folder and you can change what those who are sharing can do.

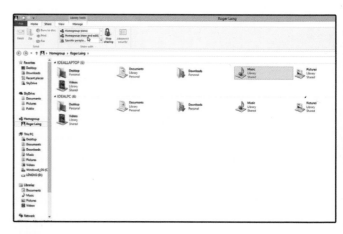

Above: Change the permissions on folders to allow them to be modified by others.

SHARING FILES AND FOLDERS

It's now no longer possible to set up HomeGroup in Windows. However, any folders or files you previously shared with HomeGroup will still be shared.

You can also still see HomeGroup (view) and HomeGroup (view and edit) in Windows. Right-click a folder in File Explorer and select Give access to. Unfortunately, if you choose either option nothing happens.

Now, if you want to share a file or folder, there are different ways to do so. To share files with people:

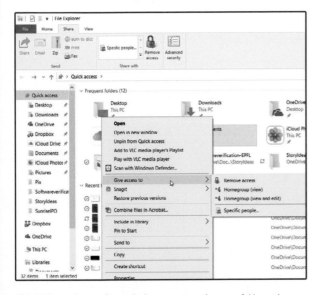

Above: Choose the specific people that you want to share your folders with.

1. Right-click on the file to share, select Give access to, then Specific people.

2. Alternatively, select the file or folder you want to share and go to the Share tab, then in the Share with section, select Specific people.

3. Start typing the name of the people you want to share the file with, select Add for each one, then press Share.

To stop sharing in File Explorer, right-click or press the files or folder and select Give access to then Remove access.

SHARING PRINTERS

Windows makes it very simple to share printers – whether it's one on your network or attached to an individual PC.

Sharing a Network Printer

This is a stand-alone printer that's not linked to a specific PC. It may be physically connected to the network by Ethernet cable or be accessed wirelessly.

Hot Tip

When you share a network printer, it is available to all the computers and devices on your network.

1. Before you can print to a network printer, you need to tell Windows that it is there, which is done through the Add Printer wizard.

2. Open the Control Panel: in Windows 7, click the Start button and select from the Start menu, while in Windows type Control Panel in the Search box on the taskbar.

3. Click Devices and Printers, then the Add a printer button on the toolbar. In the Add Printer wizard you'll see all the network printers available. Select the one you want to use and click Next.

4. If Windows can't find it, you can enter its details manually. You will need the printer's web (IP) address, which you can get from your network administrator at work or from the router (see page 136). Click The printer that I want isn't listed and, when prompted, enter the information and click Next.

5. Windows will copy the correct drivers to operate the printer. If prompted, click Install Driver to allow this. Once installed, the wizard will offer to make the printer your default one.

Above: Select the printer you wish to use.

6 Some newer printers may be automatically discovered by Windows when first connected to the network. If so, you will see the printer's icon in the Devices and Printers window.

Share Your Local Printer

If the printer is physically connected to your PC, you can still share this with others on the network. By default, everyone on the network can use your printer.

Share Your Local Printer with the Network

To share your local printer with your network, follow these steps:

1. Make sure that the printer is connected (typically, this will be through the USB port) and switched on.

2. Open the Control Panel and then the Devices and Printers tool. In the Printers and Faxes section, you should see the printer that you want to share; right-click and select Printer Properties.

3. In the Sharing tab check the box beside Share this printer and click OK.

Sharing Printers with Your HomeGroup

In earlier versions of Windows you can also share printers with your HomeGroup.

○ **Windows 8.1**: Select Settings in the Charms bar, then Change PC settings. Select Network,

Above: Share the printer that's physically connected to your PC with others on the network.

then HomeGroup and move the slider switch beside Printers from Off to On.

○ **Windows 7**: Go to the Control Panel, select HomeGroup and make sure that Printers is selected in the items that you want to share.

STREAM MEDIA ACROSS YOUR NETWORK

Why keep your music, photos and videos to yourself when you can stream them across your home network to play on your tablet, TV, Xbox, Hi-Fi speakers or other devices?

Streaming Using Windows Media Player

It's easy to stream your favourite media:

1. Launch Windows Media Player. In Windows 7, go to the Start button and click All Programs. In later versions of Windows, type Windows Media Player into the Search box on the taskbar.

2. Open it and click Library.

3. Here is where you set the options to enable other devices on your network to get access. On the toolbar, press Stream.

Above: Set up media streaming to various devices.

4. Allow Internet access to home media lets you stream music, pictures and so on to a computer outside your home, such as a friend's house, via the internet.

5. Once set up on your computer, the same settings have to be applied to the other PC.

6. Allow Remote Control of my Player lets other users push their photos, music and videos to your Windows Media Player and control playback.

7. Turn on media streaming (previously Turn on media streaming with HomeGroup... in Windows 7) lets other users and devices access the media you have on your computer. Select this and a new window opens where you can control what content is accessible.

Step 1: Select Change advanced sharing settings.

Step 2: Expand the page by clicking the arrow.

CONTENT CONTROL

When using Windows Media Player for streaming, you decide what content is shared with other computers and devices on your network. Follow these steps and keep control.

1. Go to the Control Panel and select the Network and Sharing Center, then Change advanced sharing settings.

2. Click on the arrow under All Networks to expand the page.

3. Under Media streaming, click the link to Choose media streaming options.

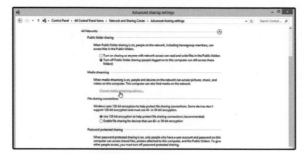

Step 3: Select Choose media streaming options.

Step 4: Choose a name for the media library.

Step 5: Decide on ratings for the content.

Step 7: Select individual devices from the list and change what they can access.

4. In the box beside Name your media library, add the label you want.

5. Select Choose default settings... and decide the Star and Parental ratings (which range from 1 to 5 stars) for the content that you want to allow to be streamed to other network computers. These star ratings are automatically assigned by online stores and third-party companies.

6. From the drop-down box, select if you want the devices to show on all networks or just the local one.

7. Select the Allow All or Block All button. In order to change what individual devices can access, select the name from the list and choose Allowed or Blocked, or click the link to Customize. Click Next and complete the wizard.

Time to Play

In Windows 7, you can only stream through Windows Media Player. That has changed in later versions of Windows, where you can play music and videos across the network directly from the Groove Music and Photos apps, as well as stream content like YouTube videos through your browsers, including Internet Explorer and Microsoft Edge.

Hot Tip

You can manually change Star and Parental ratings in Windows Media Player. Right-click the item, select rate and assign the rating you prefer (*see* pages 148–149)

Setting up Streaming Through Windows Apps

In order to do this, you'll need to have your home network set up and sharing turned on so that your PC can connect to devices, such as your TV or Xbox, on the same network. It was probably turned on when you first set up the network, but you can check by pressing the Windows key + I on the keyboard and then Change PC settings in earlier versions of Windows or opening the Control Panel in Windows 10.

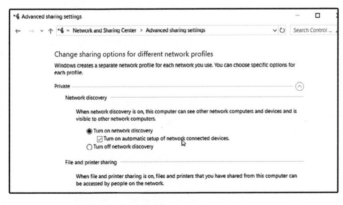

Above: Make sure Network discovery is active to find the other available devices.

1. Previously, you'd select Network and Connections, then press your network name to make sure that Find devices and content is On.

2. Now, you open Network and Sharing Center, then Advanced sharing settings. click the dropdown arrow beside Private and make sure that the options Turn on network discovery and Turn on automatic setup of network connected devices are selected.

3. You'll also need a device that can support streaming. Microsoft's Xbox is one but there are a growing number of TVs, speaker sets, tablets, smartphones and the like that can work.

Start Streaming

Follow the steps above to make sure that your PC and the device you are streaming to are both on the same network and can see each other.

1. Tap or click Connect and select the name of the device that you want to connect with and the connection should start working.

2. By default, the connected device will mirror whatever is on your screen. Press the Windows key + P (or the Project button) to open up other display modes.

Hot Tip

Open the content you want to stream with the relevant app. Built-in Windows apps like Photos, Microsoft Edge and Movies & TV can stream, but there are other third-party apps that also support this.

Casting

Launch the Microsoft Edge browser and enter the address of the site you want to cast. Once there, tap the More button to open the Options menu.

Select Cast Media to Device and select the device you want to cast to. Once connected the media should start streaming.

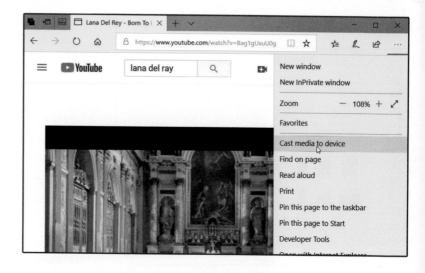

Above: Microsoft Edge allows you to stream directly from your browser to a smart TV or other device.

SHARING INFORMATION ACROSS NETWORKS

No computer is an island, and now it is easier than ever to share files and more with others, wherever they are.

Step 1: Open File Explorer and choose the folder to be shared.

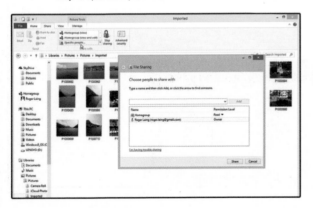

Step 2: Click Specific people to open the wizard.

SHARE WITH EVERYONE

Windows makes it easy to share with the other PC users in your home, even if they are using different versions of Windows. Just follow these steps.

1. From the desktop, open File Explorer and navigate to the folder you want to share. Select the folder in the Navigation bar and tap or click the Share tab.

2. On the Ribbon, click Specific people and the file sharing wizard opens (in Windows 7, go to the Menu bar and click the arrow beside Share with and select Specific people...).

3. You can enter a name or click the arrow to see a drop-down list of user accounts you can share with. These

will include all the user accounts on your computer and one called Everyone.

4. Select this option if you want to share with computers running a different operating system. Click Add and it will show in the panel below.

5. By default, the user accounts you share with have read-only permission. You can change this by selecting Permission Level next to Everyone and choosing Read/Write. Click Share.

6. You may be asked if you want to extend the same permissions to other users you're sharing with. You might also receive notification that the folder has been shared, with an offer to email the link to the user with whom you're sharing the folder.

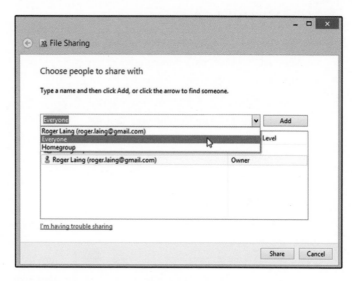

Step 3: Select a user account to share with from the drop-down menu.

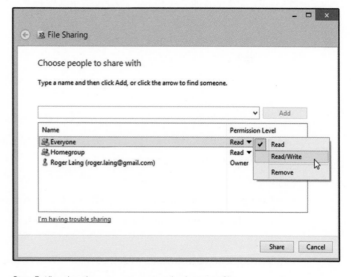

Step 5: Allow the other user accounts to make changes to files.

YOUR PC NAME

Every computer, PC and laptop alike, has a network name – technically called unique identification – so that it can be easily identified. If it's an embarrassing nickname, you might want to change it before logging your laptop on to the office network.

Finding and Changing Your Network Name

If you want to change your network name, follow these steps:

1. To find your computer's network name, select the System Window. In later versions of Windows, use the Search box to find the Control Panel and select System. In Windows 7, go to the Start menu, select Control Panel and then System.

2. Among the items there, you'll see the following:

    ○ **Computer name:** The name others see when they're browsing the network in the navigation bar.

    ○ **Full computer name:** The title given when the PC was first set up. Typically, this is your name. It can't be changed.

    ○ **Computer description:** Often left blank, it might be useful (but it's unlikely) if you have a few PCs and want to remember what makes each one different.

    ○ **Workgroup:** Often stays with that name (Workgroup); it is just the name of the local network of which the computer is part.

3. To alter the name, click Change settings and the System Properties box opens. Click the Change button and enter your new choice of name, then click OK. The change won't take effect until you restart the computer.

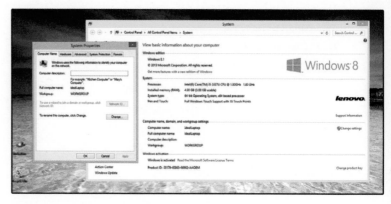

Above: When the System Properties box opens, type in the new name of your network.

SYNCING INFORMATION

You may well have a desktop PC and a laptop, not to mention a tablet or smartphone, on which you want to have the same up-to-date files or information. Fortunately, there are several cloud services to keep your digital life in sync.

OneDrive

One of the key features of the latest versions of Windows is the way OneDrive is built in. You can access it from its own Windows app, from File Explorer or through your web browser (as Windows 7 users can) by going to onedrive.live.com.

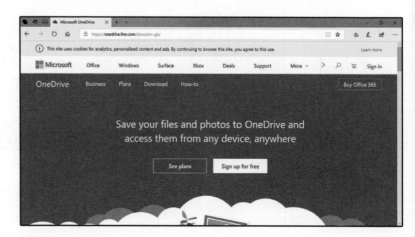

Above: One way to access OneDrive is through a web browser.

The advantage of OneDrive is that anything you upload to the cloud – documents, photos, music, and so on – can be accessed from anywhere just by logging in to the same account. This could be through your phone, Xbox or another PC. The account is free, and with it you get 5 GB of storage, with paid options to add more. As the files are synchronized with all your PCs and devices, you can be sure that you always have an up-to-date version of any file to work on.

Hot Tip

OneDrive is an online storage service. Your files and settings are stored on Microsoft's servers in the cloud. In reality, the cloud is a massive data centre in a very down-to-earth location.

Above: Upload pictures to OneDrive in order to access them from anywhere by logging in to your account.

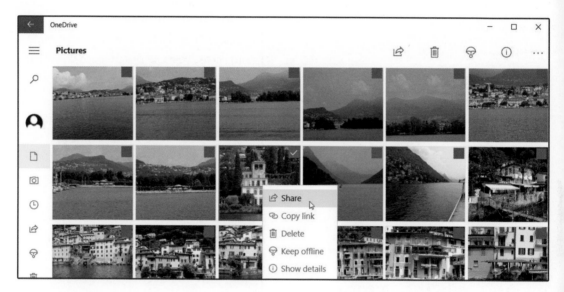

Above: To share photos, email an invite to view them on OneDrive, share on a social network or create a link to paste elsewhere.

Sharing Files and Photos

It's easy to share files – even big ones – with just the people you choose by using OneDrive. In order to do so, upload your files (depending on your plan they can be up to 20 GB in size through the app, 15 GB through a browser) to your OneDrive account, select what you want to share and choose Sharing, then choose how you want to share.

- **By email**: An invitation to come to OneDrive and view the file or photo album rather than the item itself. As you choose who receives the invitation, you can change who can share your item by removing permission later.

- **On social networks**: Create a Share link that you can choose to share on social networks like Facebook and Twitter.

- **With a link**: You can paste this into a web page or chat message.

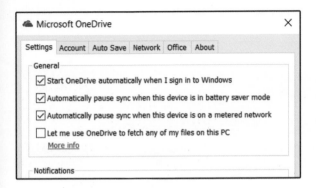

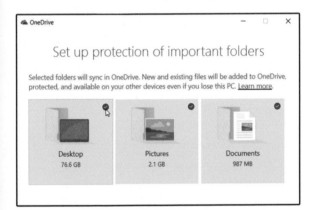

Above: Select which folders you wish to protect by automatically saving them to OneDrive.

OneDrive Settings

You can use File Explorer in Desktop mode to access your OneDrive files or download the OneDrive app that's available in the Microsoft Store.

- **Photos:** Those you take with your PC or laptop camera are saved in a folder called Camera roll. A lower resolution (smaller) copy of each photo will automatically be backed up – that is uploaded and stored – in OneDrive.

- **New documents:** Those created in programs like Word or Excel will, by default, be saved to OneDrive rather than to the hard drive of your PC. This way, they are backed up and you can access the same document and work on it from another PC or device by signing in to your OneDrive account. If you prefer, it's easy to override this when you save a document and keep it on your hard drive.

Hot Tip

You can change automatic document saving to the cloud by right-clicking the OneDrive icon in the notification area of the taskbar, clicking Settings, then Autosave and Update Folders. Uncheck the folders you don't want to autosave.

- **Choose folders to sync:**
  A backup copy of your settings is saved in the cloud, so if anything happens to your PC and you replace it, you can transfer them to a new PC just by logging in to your OneDrive account (also referred to as your Microsoft Account).

Hot Tip

You can temporarily pause OneDrive and resume syncing later. To do so right-click OneDrive in the notification area of the taskbar and click Pause syncing. Select 2, 8 or 24 hours from the dropdown list.

INTERNET SHARING

There is no shortage of cloud services like OneDrive that will let you store your files and share them between your PCs and mobile devices.

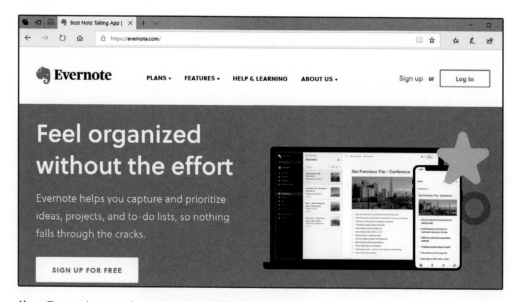

Above: There are alternative online storage services to OneDrive, such as Evernote.

Online Storage

Although not built into Windows, like OneDrive, most online storage services have Windows apps in addition to desktop programs, for users with older versions of the operating system.

- **Services to try**: Among the best-known services are: Dropbox, Evernote, Apple's iCloud, Google Drive and SugarSync.

- **Automatic syncing**: The exact features differ, but generally they set up a folder on your computer. Anything added to this will be synced with the online service so that it can then be shared with any other device that has the same software installed.

- **Free accounts**: Most services offer free accounts, with storage from 5 to 15 GB, with the option and hope that you will upgrade to the premium features of their paid-for services.

USING PUBLIC NETWORKS

Windows can help to protect your PC when you access the internet from a hotel, airport or other public place.

Setting Your Network Profile

With a laptop computer, you may connect to several different networks over the course of a day, week or month. But all networks are not equal. While you may want to share files and information over your home or work networks, you don't want the person in the coffee shop sitting next to you having the same access. Follow these steps to avoid sharing your information.

1. Windows sets up a network profile the first time you connect to a specific network by asking if you want to enable sharing and automatically connect to other devices (*see* pages 134–135).

2. According to your answer, Windows will change the settings related to sharing.

○ **Say Yes and Windows sets up a private network:** This is for trusted networks like your home or office. Network discovery is turned on so you can see all the other computers and devices, such as printers, external hard drives, etc., that are on the same network. Other users can share files on your PC.

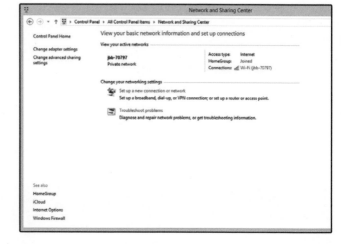

Above: Set up private networks for trusted locations.

○ **Say No and network discovery is turned off:** Your computer is not visible or accessible to other users. This is best when you are in a public place, such as a bar, restaurant or airport.

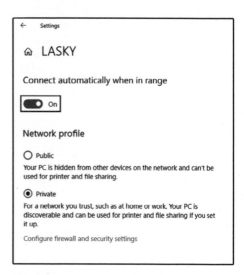

Above: Change your network profile to Private in less secure, public places.

> **Hot Tip**
>
> Change your network profile by pressing the Windows key + I, then selecting Network & Internet. Tap or click Change connection properties and then change your network profile to Public or Private, as required.

MOBILE INTERNET

The portability of a laptop PC is great, as you can use it wherever you are: at a friend's house or in the park. However, as so much of life today is played out online, it's not that practical without an internet connection.

Smartphone Tethering

It sounds painful – and it could be if you're not on an unlimited data plan for your mobile. Basically, it allows you to set up your own Personal Hotspot – or access point – to the Internet by sharing your smartphone's connection. Mobile phone operators may charge extra to allow this service and there may also be extra usage costs if you're not on an all-you-can-download data plan. You can connect laptop and phone in the following ways:

Above: It is possible to share your smartphone's Wi-Fi connection with your PC.

- ○ **Wi-Fi**: Select the phone name in the network settings on your computer and, when prompted, enter the password, which you can find in the Settings on your phone.

- ○ **Bluetooth**: Pair the smartphone and computer like any other Bluetooth device. You may have to enter a code displayed on the laptop screen into the smartphone settings.

- ○ **USB**: Connect the smartphone to the laptop by USB cable and it should appear in the network settings.

Mobile Modem

Tablet PCs often come with space to insert a mobile phone-style SIM card that gives access to the internet. On laptops or tablets without SIM support, the answer is a mobile modem. Typically, the modems will plug into the laptop through the USB port or connect wirelessly via Wi-Fi or Bluetooth.

In order to connect to the internet, you generally have to launch a program supplied with the modem that handles the connection. The quality and speed of the connection will vary greatly, just like that for any mobile device.

In order to hook up several devices to the internet, such as your smartphone, tablet and laptop, there are mobile hotspots. These small wireless routers (also referred to as MiFi, which is short for My Wi-Fi) are provided by mobile operators to supply Internet access for anything from five to 10 devices at the same time.

Hot Tip

The price of the modem and the cost of your data usage will vary according to the mobile operator providing the service.

Above: Small wireless routers known as MiFi devices can support internet access to multiple devices at the same time.

PROTECTION

BACKING UP

There's only one real precaution you can take against losing all your personal data if your PC breaks down: back up everything regularly.

WHEN AND WHERE TO BACK UP

There's not much point in backing up your files to the same PC because if it fails, both originals and copies will be lost. Fortunately, inexpensive, high-capacity external drives are readily available or, alternatively, you can back up online.

Back up to an External Drive

The simplest form of backup is to a local, external drive. Despite their small physical size, even portable backup drives can store between 1–2 terabytes (TB) of data, with compact desktop models storing up to 4 TB.

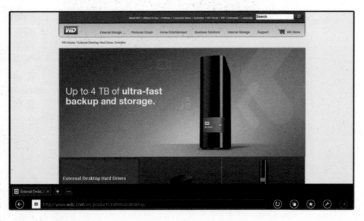

Most drives connect via the USB port. If you have a USB 3.0 port, it is better to choose a drive which supports it because it will enable you to back up high volumes of data, faster. There are also wireless drives.

Most drives come with the manufacturer's choice of backup software, which, once

Above: External drives may look small, but they can hold a large amount of data.

installed and configured, will run automatically. Alternatively, you can use the backup programs in Windows (see page 168) or commercial backup programs, which offer additional features.

Some are the traditional file-and-folder backup programs (e.g. Rebit) which make copies of your files in the background, whereas other drive-imaging applications, like Acronic Disk Director, take a snapshot of the entire drive. As the image includes the system files, you can burn it to a DVD or store it on the network to use as a start-up drive in an emergency.

With a home network, you could also back up to a networked drive.

Back up to the Cloud

The introduction of fast broadband internet connections with unlimited data plans has led to a number of online (cloud) backup services.

Above: CrashPlan is a specialist provider for backing up files online.

Typically, you download and install the software from the backup provider and then tell it which files, folders or drives you want to include. The software will run in the background, monitoring the locations you've chosen and uploading any changes virtually instantly. This way, different versions of the same file are backed up and can be retrieved.

Subscription costs vary according to the space you want, the number of computers you're backing up and for how long you're willing to sign up.

Hot Tip

While online storage services like Dropbox and Google Drive could be used for backup, specialist backup providers, such as CrashPlan, Backblaze and Mozy, offer automatic backup that's incremental, i.e., after the initial lengthy backup, only new or changed files are uploaded.

HOW TO BACK UP

Such is the importance of backup that it is built into Windows and the system will alert you, through the Action Center, if it is not set up.

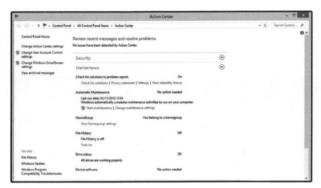

Above: File History must be turned on to back up files automatically.

Hot Tip

In order to reduce the size of your backups, don't include items, such as your music files, which may already be backed up through one of the online music services.

File History

Backup in Windows has been rechristened File History, as you can back up not only your files but also different versions of individual files. Once File History is turned on, the backup runs automatically, provided that the location where you're storing the copies is available.

Step 1: Select File History from the Control Panel.

SETTING UP FILE HISTORY

The easiest way to set up File History is through the desktop app Control Panel, as it gives you the most options.

1. Type Control Panel in the Search box. Select the app from the panel that opens and then File History.

2. When you first open it, Windows will search for a suitable drive to use for backups. It recommends an external hard drive or you can choose a network location, such as a folder on another computer.

3. Click Select a network location, then Add network location. Backups will be placed in a folder called File History on the target drive you've selected.

4. File History will only back up files in certain folders, i.e. your libraries plus contacts, favourites and desktop. If you want to back up other files outside of these, then put them – or a copy – in one of the Libraries.

5. Select Exclude folders from the left-hand side menu, then click Add to browse your folders and libraries, and select those you don't wish to back up. Press Save changes.

6. Click Advanced Settings to set more backup options.

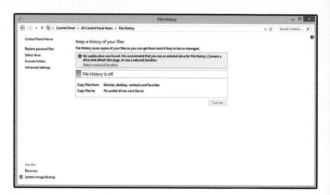

Step 2: Windows will search for a location to save back up files to.

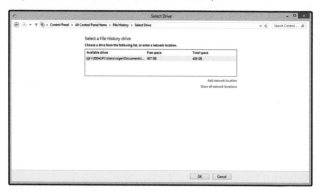

Step 3: Select Add network location to choose where backups will go.

Step 5: Exclude certain folders from being automatically backed up.

- **Save copies of files**: Lets you choose how frequently file copies are made, which can be the default (every hour) or range from every 10 minutes to daily.

Step 6: Advanced Settings offers more backup options.

Step 7: Each user will have to turn on File History in their own account.

- **Size of offline cache**: The amount of space that can be used for backups on the disk that's storing them; the default is five per cent.

- **Keep saved versions**: Sets how long to keep the different versions – from the default (for ever) to when space is needed.

7. Click the Turn on button to activate File History and it will automatically back up files to the schedule you set. It will, however, only back up files on your user account. If there are other people using the PC, who have separate user accounts, they will have to turn on File History independently.

Hot Tip

Although Libraries used to be shown by default in File Explorer, they are not now. In order to turn them on, go to the View tab, click the arrow beside Navigation pane and select Show Libraries.

Back up in Windows 7

Automatic – or manual – backup is easy to set up in Windows 7.

1. Click the Start button, select Control Panel, then Backup and Restore.

2. Click Set up backup and follow the wizard to configure backup.

3. After the first full backup, only new or altered files will be backed up.

4. Apart from the scheduled backups, you can run one any time by clicking Back up now.

RESTORE FILES AND BACKUPS

Should disaster strike, it's possible to restore the original files or folders and even roll back your system to a version that you know works.

1. Go to File History in the Control Panel.

2. Click Restore personal files to open the wizard.

3. Select the Libraries and folders you want to restore.

Step 2: Click Restore personal files to start the wizard.

Step 3: Select which files to restore.

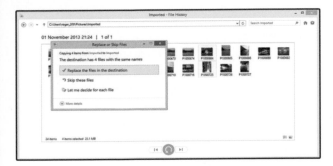

Step 7: Select Replace the files in the destination.

Step 8: The copied over content will now be displayed.

4. If you just want to restore a file, browse to its location and select it. If there are several files, press and hold Ctrl as you click on each one.

5. In order to restore files to a different location, select them, click the Options button (the small cog wheel on the top right) and then select Restore to.

6. Press the green button to start the process.

7. Confirm you want to Replace the files in the destination with your backup.

8. Once finished, File Explorer will open to show all the content that has been copied over.

Restore Backups in Windows 7

You can restore individual files or all the files that you have backed up.

1. Go to Backup and Restore in the Control Panel.
2. Restore my files opens the backup.
3. Select Browse for folders if you want to restore groups of files. If you want to copy over individual files, then click Browse for files.
4. If you want to restore files created on another computer running Windows, click Select another backup to restore files from and follow the steps in the wizard.

SYSTEM RESTORE

Rather than just your files and folders, Windows will take snapshots of your entire system so that you can restore your PC to a previously working state in the event of a problem.

System Restore Points

A longtime feature of Windows, System Restore is turned on by default and works automatically in the background. Every time you make a significant change to your system, such as installing new software, it creates a restore point. If your PC starts behaving badly, you can roll back the system to a time when it was working well.

Restoring Your System

Here is how to restore your system.

1. Launch the System Restore wizard by launching the Control Panel and selecting System. In Windows 7, go to the Control Panel and select System.

2. Click the System protection link.

Above: If a problem occurs, the entire computer system can be restored.

3. The System Properties box will open and under Protection Settings, you can see which drives are protected.

4. In order to undo system changes, click the System Restore button, which launches the wizard.

5. The most recent restore point is shown. Select that and click Scan for affected programs to see the changes that will be made.

6. Click Next and you're prompted to confirm the restore point. Click Finish to start the process.

PROTECT YOUR PC

Your PC comes with its own defences to protect you from the threat of a virus attack and other malware. You can also lock the computer to prevent unauthorized access to your personal files.

SECURITY PROGRAMS

With each version of Windows, the built-in security programs have been improved to protect your PC from viruses, spyware, malware and worse.

Security and Maintenance

Part of the Control Panel, Security and Maintenance monitors Windows and will alert you as soon as it notices a problem. Previously, it would do so by showing a red cross beside a white flag on the Taskbar. Now these alerts, along with other system notifications, are shown in the Action Center.

Above: Click the Action Center icon on the Taskbar to open it.

- **Open Action Center:** Click the icon on the far right-hand side of the Taskbar. You can also open the Security and Maintenance Center directly through the Control Panel.

Secuity and maintenance problems are colour-coded to show their severity.

- **Red:** Critical problems that need immediate attention, such as an issue detected with virus protection or the firewall.

- **Amber**: Issues that you should look at soon, such as setting up backup.

Click the button beside each message and Windows will attempt to fix the problem automatically or will take you to a solution page to help you find the answer.

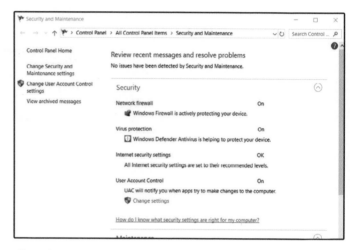

Malware Protection

- **Computer viruses**: Just like the human kind, these spread

Above: The Security and Maintenance center will display any problems and offer the opportunity to fix them.

rapidly and you're not aware you're infected until it's too late. They are a type of malware – short for malicious software – that tries to disrupt normal computer operations, can steal your data, trash your hard drive and use your computer to infect others.

- **Antivirus program**: The best inoculation against infection is an antivirus program, which will check your PC against a constantly evolving list of the latest bugs.

- **Spyware**: One of the worst kinds of malware is spyware, which is often unknowingly downloaded to your PC, through a web browser, email and the like. These programs monitor what you do and can gather your passwords and other sensitive information. In order to combat them, you need anti-spyware software.

Hot Tip

There are many commercial antivirus and anti-spyware programs from companies such as McAfee, AVG and Symantec. Windows Defender doesn't have many of their features, such as antispam or ad blockers, but is a good free solution.

○ **Defender**: In previous versions of Windows, Defender was just for protection against spyware. For antivirus protection, users could download Microsoft Security Essentials. Now the two have been brought together so that Defender protects against viruses and spyware, as well as maintaining the health of your device.

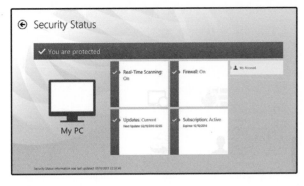

Above: Commercial antivirus and anti-spyware software offers many features to keep computers safe.

USING WINDOWS DEFENDER

Windows Defender protects against viruses and spyware, so it is great to have this on your PC to guard you in case of attack.

1. To open Windows Defender Security Center, go to the Start screen, type 'defender' and select it in the search results (in Windows 7, go to the Start menu, select Control Panel and then Windows Defender).

2. Select Virus & threat protection and make sure that the switch under Real-time protection is set to On. In Windows 7, select Tools, then Options.

3. Go to the Home tab to see a colour-coded overview of the state of your entire system, covering everything from Firewall & network protection to App & browser control and Device security: green means all is OK, orange shows that there are warnings you need to act on and red shows problems were found.

4. Windows Defender automatically scans your system. When a threat is detected, it is isolated and put into 'quarantine', and you are sent an alert.

5. In order to review it and decide whether you want to remove it completely, go to Threat History in Windows Defender, choose Quarantined threats, then View details. Check any item you want to clear from your PC and click Remove.

Using Windows Firewall

As further protection for your PC, Windows Firewall helps to block suspicious programs from your computer, while letting safe apps communicate freely across your network and with the internet. When you install a program, it will also ask for access through the firewall to your network and the internet.

Above: Windows Defender shows your Security at a glance.

If Windows Firewall suspects a program, you will receive a Security Alert saying it has blocked some feature of the app and asking which network profile you wish to apply for this program: Private to give trusted access to your Home or Work network or Public for restricted access if you are in a public place.

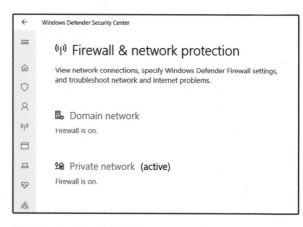

Above: Windows Firewall has different settings for different network types.

> ## Hot Tip
> Windows Firewall is turned on by default, but it applies its own set of rules so that you can do the things you expect, such as browse the internet, chat, share files on the network, etc.

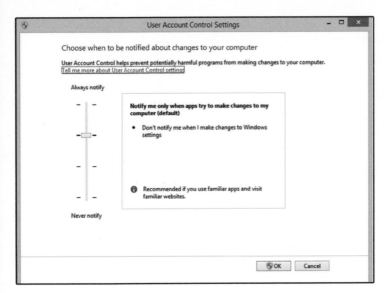

User Account Control

Like Windows Firewall, this works in the background and helps to stop viruses or malware making unauthorized changes to your PC. The default setting is that you'll only see it when new software is installed or a program tries to make changes to Windows, such as restoring backed-up files.

Above: User Account Control can be set to only prompt for permission at certain times.

User Account Control launches a prompt box asking if you want to allow the changes. Click Yes and they go ahead; select No and no changes are made.

Hot Tip

Change when you get alerts. Go to the Control Panel, then User Accounts and click or tap Change User Account control settings, and set the slider to the level of protection you want.

LOCK YOUR PC

In order to prevent prying eyes when you leave your computer, it's a good idea to lock your system so that anyone wanting access will have to sign in.

The Lock Screen

The Lock screen can be customized to display your photos – even a slideshow, the number of emails waiting, and so on – when your system is locked. In order to personalize it, open Windows Settings, choose Personalization and then select Lock screen.

Manually Lock Your Computer

There are three ways to lock your computer manually.

1. Go to the Start screen, click your user account on the left and select Lock.

2. Press Ctrl + Alt + Delete and select Lock.

3. Press the Windows key + L on the keyboard.

Automatically Lock Your Computer

A screensaver will lock your computer after a period of inactivity.

Above: Different images can be chosen to be displayed on the Lock screen.

1. Press the Windows key + I to open Windows Settings and then select Personalization, Lock Screen and then Screen Saver Settings.

2. Choose a screensaver from the drop-down list. In the box next to Wait, select how long a period of inactivity you want (measured in minutes) before the PC locks.

3. Check the box beside On resume, display logon screen and click OK.

SAFETY ONLINE

For all the benefits of the internet in spreading knowledge and resolving arguments in the pub, there are dangers out there, which are avoidable with suitable precautions.

AVOIDING ONLINE SCAMS

Chances are high that you'll have received a fake email or website link that attempted to get you to reveal your private information. Windows has tools to help protect you against these phishing threats.

Hot Tip

SmartScreen compares web addresses with a known list of fraudulent sites. If there's a match, a warning notice advises you that the site has been reported as unsafe and not to continue.

Above: Turn on SmartScreen in Microsoft Edge to provide extra defence against online threats.

Safe Browsing

If Microsoft Edge is your web browser, check that the SmartScreen filter is turned on. When running Edge on the desktop, click the More button (three dots). Choose Settings and then scroll down and select View advanced settings. Scroll to the bottom and make sure that Help protect me from malicious sites and downloads with Windows Defender SmartScreen is turned on.

PARENTAL CONTROLS

Although computers are a part of everyday life for children, parental controls can help to keep them safe online, and regulate which apps they can use and for how long.

Family Safety

This is a built-in feature for Windows that helps parents control how their children use the computer.

1. To turn it on, you first have to set up a separate user account for the child. Do this in Windows by pressing the Windows key + I to open Windows Settings, then choose Accounts. Select Family & other people, then click the + sign beside Add a family member.

2. In the screen that opens, click Add a child's account. If they already have an email address, or one linked to a Microsoft account, enter that. Otherwise, you can set one up on their behalf.

3. Use this last option, add a username and password, and the account is set up. Family Safety is turned on by default, but you need to edit the account to add any controls.

Above: Set up separate accounts for children and control their settings.

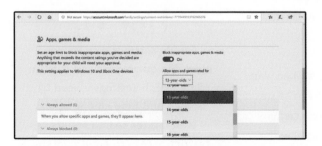

Above: You can make sure that your children can only access age-appropriate content.

Setting up Safe Accounts

In order to set up Family Safety controls, click the link to Manage family settings online. Sign in and you can manage your child's activity online. There are several types of settings you can change:

Device limits

Use one schedule for all devices

On

Xbox One and Winows 10 devices

How much time can your child have each day across all of their devices, and when can they use them? ⑦

Day	Time limit	12 am	4 am	8 am	12 pm	4 pm	8 pm
Sunday	Max scheduled ⌄						
Monday	Max scheduled ⌄						
Tuesday	Max scheduled ⌄						
Wednesday	Max scheduled ⌄						

Left: Limit screen time for your children by setting time restrictions.

1. **Web filtering:** You can prevent your child from accessing inappropriate apps, games and media – any content in fact that you feel may not be suitable:

○ Select Content restrictions from the top of the Windows Family Safety section.

○ Turn on Needs adult approval to buy things to control what your child can purchase in the Microsoft Store. You can also get an email sent to you whenever your child buys something.

○ In the next section you can set an age limit for content. Turn on the switch to Block inappropriate apps, games & media. In the dropdown box below select the age of your child. They will only be allowed to use apps and games that are rated suitable for their age.

2. **Time limits:** These set the times when your child can use the computer, and can be set for each day of the week and for a certain number of hours per day. You can alter the times for weekdays and weekends.

Hot Tip

Family settings also let you block file downloads and turn on SafeSearch settings – used by Google and Bing among others – which filter search results to restrict access to adult content.

3. **Game and Microsoft Store app restrictions**: The violent nature of some games makes this an important feature, particularly for protecting younger children. You can Always allow or Always block individual games as well as use the browser to block websites you believe are unsuitable for their age.

4. **Restrict spending**: Limit how much your children can spend on buying apps, games, music and other content through Windows and the Microsoft Store.

Parental Controls in Windows 7

These are similar to those in Windows now and you can download additional controls from third parties. In order to access them, go to the Control Panel and select Parental controls.

Above: If taking a laptop on a flight, Airplane mode should be switched on.

Safety When Flying

Even if your laptop has a switch for turning off wireless communications, as is still necessary on many flights, it's safer to put your PC into Airplane mode. This cuts off all Wi-Fi, mobile broadband, Bluetooth, etc. while still enabling you to use the PC.

To activate it, click the Action Center logo on the far-right of the Taskbar. Click or tap the control marked Airplane mode to toggle it on or off.

KEEP YOUR DATA SAFE

From physical security to encrypting your files so they are unreadable by anyone without the key, there are precautions to take in order to protect your personal information.

SECURE YOUR PC

In order to avoid your laptop or PC being physically stolen, the best thing to do is to lock it down. You can secure it to the desk, at home or in the office. Most computers will have a universal slot to which you can fasten the lock, if not then there are other ways to attach them.

PASSWORDS

No matter how good the security programs on your PC, you are still vulnerable to attack if you do not regularly review and change your passwords.

Good Password Habits

Get into the following habits to protect your personal data:

1.   Use secure passwords that are at least eight characters long. They should contain a mix of letters, both upper- and lower-case, and numbers.

2.   Don't always use the same one, because if it's hacked or accidentally discovered, then you have no security. If it is difficult to remember all your passwords, use a password manager. Programs like 1Password (www.agilebits.com) create and store passwords so that all you have to remember is the master password.

3.   In order to change your password, press the Windows key + I to open Windows Settings, then Accounts, Sign-in options and, under Password, click Change. Enter your existing

Above: A good safety tip is to regularly change passwords.

password in the window that opens and you're taken to the online section where you can change the password you want.

4. Change your passwords regularly; in Windows, you can force yourself to adopt a new one every 72 days by ticking the box in the Change your password section online.

Encrypt Your Data

Windows will automatically encrypt data on your hard drive so that, if your laptop or PC is stolen, your files are still safe. This feature is only available if you sign in using your Microsoft account and if you have a compatible Windows device. If you're running an earlier version of Windows or your PC doesn't support device encryption, then there are other programs available, such as VeraCrypt, which is free.

Hot Tip

In Sign-in options, you can select to have a picture password – which can be set up with a mouse but is more suitable for touch, as it involves three taps or clicks on a photo – or a mobile-style four-digit PIN.

Above: It is possible to set up certain gestures on a picture as a password.

TOUCH

TOUCH-SCREEN PCs

As the first operating system designed to work across PCs, tablets and smartphones, Windows lets you control your devices by touching or tapping rather than using the mouse.

TABLET PCs

Tablet PCs come in a variety of styles, but are distinguished by the fact that they can all be operated by touch, with the finger or stylus replacing the mouse.

Different Types of Tablet PCs

- **Convertibles**: The most common type. They are laptops with a twist, since the screen can be swivelled or slid over the keyboard to turn it into a tablet.

- **Slate models**: Conventional all-in-one touch screens without a keyboard.

- **Hybrids**: May have a detachable or retractable keyboard, but are both a tablet (with portable touch screen) and PC (running Windows).

Right: The Lenovo Thinkpad Twist is an example of a convertible PC.

What to Look for in a Tablet PC

○ **Windows version**: Previously, there was a special version of Windows for tablet PCs. Now Windows is a universal operating system. The same version of Windows you use on your PC also works on tablets.

○ **Screen size**: If you're planning to use one of the hybrid tablet PCs that can be the equal of a laptop, then you want a reasonable size screen – typically 13.3 in/33.7 cm. However, if you want it primarily for going on social networks or looking at photos, then a smaller screen is perfectly acceptable.

Above: Most Windows tablets have the minimum necessary screen resolution for snapping apps.

○ **Screen resolution**: A clear, sharp picture is a must for reading on-screen, playing games or watching movies. While some Windows tablets support resolutions up to 3840 x 2160 most are able to dock – snap – apps beside each other.

○ **Flexibility**: Make sure you're comfortable with the way the screen turns from laptop into tablet, as with some, the keyboard lifts off completely, while others twist round. For example, the Lenovo Yoga has four different positions: normal clamshell notebook mode; stand mode, with the screen tilted up and keyboard flat like a book stand; tablet mode with the screen folded over the keyboard; and tent mode, which is good for presentations.

Left: The Lenovo Yoga 13 can take four different positions, to work as either a laptop or a tablet.

- **Hard-disk space:** In order to maintain lightness, most tablet PCs won't have the large hard drives that you'll find in desktops. Mostly they range up to 256 GB, and about 13 GB of that will be taken up by Windows and various recovery tools.

SENSORS

Tablet PCs come with a range of sensors that help them to adapt to their surroundings. They can also be used by apps to provide additional features.

Light Sensor

Little more than a dot on the front panel, this checks the ambient light, i.e., the light around you, and will brighten or dim the screen accordingly. It's designed to make the screen easier to view

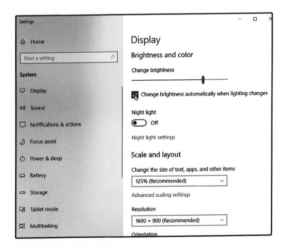

Above: Set the brightness to adapt to the surrounding light.

and save battery power. You can set Windows to change the screen's brightness automatically when the lighting around you changes.

1. Press the Windows key + I to open Windows Settings, then Display.

2. Under Brightness, tick the box beside Change brightness automatically when lighting changes.

3. You can still adjust brightness manually by pressing the Action Center icon and selecting the Brightness control. As you press it moves between settings from darkest to brightest.

Above: Screen brightness can be adjusted manually using the quick action tile in the Action Center.

Accelerometer: Rotation Sensor

This responds to the way you're holding the screen so that, when you turn it, the contents change orientation as well. However, there may be times when you prefer to keep what you're viewing, such as an ebook or web page, in landscape or portrait mode. Follow these steps to turn on the lock.

1. Click or tap the Action Center icon in the right-hand corner of the Taskbar.

Above: To prevent the screen from changing orientation when the tablet is moved, turn on the Rotation Lock.

2. Tap the Rotation Lock button at the top to toggle it on or off (on some tablet PCs, there is a dedicated button on the side that you press to switch the lock on and off).

Since it detects motion, the accelerometer is also used by some apps, particularly games, to let the user tilt and rotate the screen to control the action.

USING MULTIPLE MONITORS

It is now even easier to set up Windows to work across more than one monitor. You could, for example, create a presentation on your tablet PC and, when you want to see it on a larger scale, view it on your desktop's big screen.

Above: There are various ports at the back of the monitor for connecting to a PC.

What You Need

1. Two monitors, which could be a widescreen touch panel and ordinary monitor, tablet PC and desktop screen, or a similar combination.

2. Your desktop PC needs a video card with preferably two ports – VGA, DVI or HDMI – and corresponding ports on each of the monitors. You then connect them using the relevant cable. If you have just one DVI port, it's possible to get a cable that will split the signal and connect to two monitors.

Setting up the Display

Once your monitors are physically connected, you can set up what's seen on screen – either in Modern (Metro) or desktop view.

○ **Modern view**: In this view, click or tap the Action Center icon in the right-hand corner of the Taskbar, then press the Project button. There are four options:

1. **PC screen only**: Leaves the second monitor blank.

2. **Duplicate**: Shows the same on both screens.

3. **Extend**: Everything is spread over both screens and you can drag and drop items between them.

4. **Second screen only**: Makes the original monitor blank and uses only the other screen.

Above: Selecting PC screen only means everything will appear on the PC screen, but the second monitor will be blank.

○ **Desktop view:** In this view, you do as previously in Windows 7: select Control Panel, then Display, and make your choice from the four options (as listed above).

Changing Display Options

1. Open the Control Panel in Desktop mode and select Windows Mobility Center.

2. In the window that opens you can control different options for both displays, including their relative position. You can also separately alter brightness and screen orientation.

Hot Tip

You can choose whether the taskbar is shown on both screens or just one by pressing the Windows key + I to open Settings, then choose Personalization. Select Taskbar and, under Multiple displays, check the box beside Show taskbar on all displays.

SETTING UP TOUCH

Although it is switched on by default, and can't be turned off, there are settings you can change to improve the responsiveness of your touch screen.

Check You Have a Touch Screen

If you think your laptop or monitor should respond to touch but doesn't, Windows can verify that it is a touch screen.

1. Press the Windows key + I to open Windows Settings, then System. Select About and scroll to Device specifications.

2. Under Pen and touch, it shows whether your screen has Windows touch support and, if it does, the number of touch points it has.

3. If it does support touch but this isn't working, check on the manufacturer's website for an up-to-date driver.

Above: The higher the number of touch points, the more points of contact the screen recognizes.

Setting up Your Touch Screen

In order to improve the responsiveness of your touch screen, you should calibrate it.

1. Press the Windows key + I to open Windows Settings and search for Calibrate.

2. Select Calibrate the screen for pen or touch input, which opens the Tablet PC Settings.

3. Choose the screen to use, if there's more than one available, and follow the on-screen instructions.

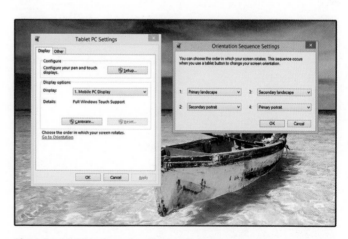

4. In order to calibrate the screen, you'll be asked to touch various points.

5. If your screen rotates, select Go to orientation to choose how it changes when moved.

Above: It is possible to change the calibration of how the screen rotates.

Using a Pen

Rather than using a finger to press the screen, some tablets come with a stylus – also known as a pen or, more technically, a digitizer. Simple to use, its main actions are the following:

- **Point**: Point the pen at the screen without touching.

- **Click**: Tap the pen on screen.

- **Double-click**: Tap the pen twice on the same spot.

- **Drag**: Touch the screen with the pen and drag it round.

USING TOUCH SCREENS

It's only through touch that you get the full Windows experience, and it opens up a completely different world of computing.

NAVIGATION BY TOUCH

With Windows touch, your fingers take over from the mouse and open up new ways of moving around your PC and controlling apps.

Single-touch Gestures

Tap once: Equivalent to left-clicking with the mouse; use it to open an app, follow a link or similar.

Press and hold: Press down and leave your finger there for a moment. This is equivalent to right-clicking with the mouse, and it allows you to open pop-up menus and get more information before selecting an action.

Slide: Dragging your finger across the screen is similar to clicking and holding with the mouse. It lets you pan or scroll through a list or web pages and, in some apps, you can also use it to move an object or for drawing and writing.

Swipe: Move the finger from the edge of the screen inwards, towards the centre.

Swipe from top or bottom edge: Similar to right-clicking in an app, it shows app commands like save, edit and delete. This will also dock or close an app that's open.

Swipe from left: Displays the apps currently running in the background.

Swipe from right: Like moving your mouse pointer to the lower-left corner, it opens the Charms bar.

Multi-touch Gestures

Pinch: Touch the screen with two fingers and move them together to zoom in or apart to zoom out. It is useful in apps like Maps, when you want to view a location close up or zoom out to see the local area. It can also be used to jump to the beginning or end of a list.

Rotate: Place two or more fingers on the screen and turn your hand to rotate an object. This only works in apps that support it.

CHANGING TOUCH SETTINGS

The manufacturer of your touch device may offer a wider range of settings that you can customize, but there are some you can change with Windows.

Swap Menu Location

If you're left-handed, you'll have a clearer view of the menus if they appear on the right-hand side and vice versa. To change where the menu appears, go to the

Control Panel and select Tablet PC Settings. Tap the Other tab. In the Handedness section, tell Windows which is your favoured hand and it alters the side where the menu appears.

ADJUSTING TOUCH ACTIONS

It's simple to adjust the touch actions of your computer; just follow these steps.

1. On the Other tab in Tablet PC Settings, click the link to Go to Pen and Touch.

2. Here, you can change how long it is before Windows responds to your touch.

3. For example, if you wanted Windows to register a double-tap when there's a longer period between the two taps, then select Double-tap and then Settings.

4. Adjust the speed bar accordingly. Similarly, if you tend to wander off the spot when you double-tap, you can use the Spatial tolerance slider to compensate.

Step 1: Click Go to Pen and Touch.

Step 3: Select Double-tap.

Step 4: Adjust the speed bar.

ON-SCREEN KEYBOARDS

For touch typing, there are different types of on-screen keyboard that make it easier to enter the information you want.

Using the Touch Keyboard

In Tablet mode, simply tap the screen where you want to enter the text and the keyboard will appear. In order to close it, tap outside the text box. On the desktop, tap the touch keyboard icon on the taskbar and, to close it, tap the X in the top-right corner.

Step 1: Open the touch keyboard.

Step 2: Select the preferred keyboard layout.

Change the Layout

1. Open the touch keyboard as previously explained.

2. Tap the language icon on the lower-right side and select the keyboard layout for the language you want.

3. Tap the small keyboard icon to change the size and position of the keyboard. For example, press the thumb keyboard layout that splits the keys and places them either side of the screen. This is designed to make it easier and more comfortable to enter text when you're standing or holding the tablet with both hands.

4. Tap the other icons to see the different types of touch keyboard available. Some will take up most of the screen but there is one smaller keyboard which sits in the middle.

Step 3: The thumb keyboard makes it easier to enter text when you're standing.

5. The touch keyboard has fewer keys on display so they can be as large as possible for easier tapping.

6. In order to access shortcuts on the standard touch keyboard, press Ctrl and you'll see some of the keys change. For example, press Ctrl and Copy appears over the letter C, so just as on a normal keyboard, you can press Ctrl + C to copy the text.

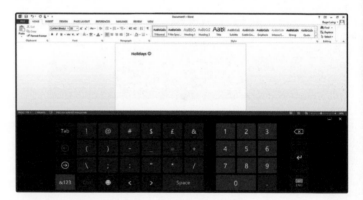

Step 7: Pressing the &123 key will switch to the numeric keypad.

7. In order to access the numeric keypad and other symbol keys, press the &123 key.

Hot Tip

A quick way to add numbers on the touch keyboard is to press and hold one of the letter keys in the top row and slide up to the number. The number attached to the key is shown in the top-left corner.

Get the Full Windows Keyboard

Previously, if you wanted your touch keyboard to have all the features of the standard desktop-style keyboard you had to activate the option in the Typing section of Settings.

1. Now a full touch keyboard – complete with Windows key, function keys and arrow keys – is built-in.

Above: If you prefer to use the full desktop-style keyboard, there is an option to do this.

Above: The touch keyboard comes with a range of emoticons to express exactly how you feel.

2. Press the Touch keyboard icon on the Taskbar, then the small keyboard icon in the left-hand corner and choose the keyboard layout in the top right corner.

3. Now you have a fully functioning Windows keyboard. But remember, it does make for more cramped typing.

Emoticons

Expressing your emotions to your friends in emails, chat, and so on is a lot easier with the touch keyboard, as it has its own smileys key. Press this and you can access dozens of smileys gathered under different headings, such as food, weather, etc. However, in order to be sure that they show up as intended on your friends' computers – especially if they're not running Windows – it's advisable to use the text-based smileys, including the original smiley face made up from a colon, dash and right parenthesis.

WRITING BY HAND

You can write (or draw) on screen and Windows will translate it into meaningful text or an image, which you can edit.

Using Handwriting Mode

If you are using a touch screen, you can switch to writing by hand (or finger, at least).

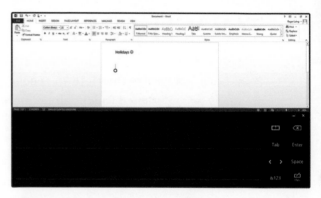

Above: In handwriting mode, you can use your finger to write with instead of typing with a keyboard.

1. Tap where you want to enter your text, e.g., in an email, Word document or a note in the Windows Journal app.

2. The keyboard appears. Tap the Switch keyboard icon and select the Stylus option (with its icon of a screen and pen).

3. The handwriting panel opens and you can begin writing. You can use cursive writing or block letters, or a combination of the two. As you do, Windows shows what it thinks you're writing. If it's correct, tap the Insert button.

4. If the word isn't recognized correctly, and you haven't pressed the Insert button, change it by drawing a line through the word.

5. If the words have already been inserted in the text box on screen, highlight what's wrong by dragging your finger or stylus across it. It should appear in the handwriting box and you can draw a line through it to delete and correct it.

6. In order to correct a single letter in a word, tap the word and the letters are spaced out. Write the correct letter over the wrong one and it will be replaced.

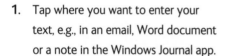

Hot Tip

Forgotten how to edit your handwritten text? Click the question mark and there are four animations available to show you how to correct, delete, split or join letters and words.

TOUCH APPS

From built-in apps like OneNote to special versions of desktop programs, there are many apps designed to let you do more on your tablet PC.

WINDOWS TOUCH APPS

There are several ready-made apps to help you take advantage of the touch features in Windows.

Windows Journal

This note-taking app, which looks like a pad of ruled paper, appeared in earlier versions of Windows. No longer automatically installed, it is still possible to download it from Microsoft.

1. In Windows 8.1, open the Search bar by pressing the Windows key + S, type in 'Windows Journal' and select from the results.

2. In Windows 7, go to the Start menu, All Programs, Accessories, Tablet PC and Windows Journal.

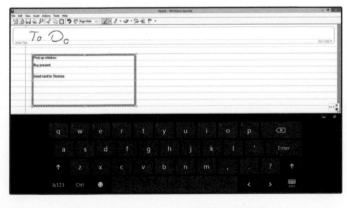

3. Once the app starts, you can write a quick note by tapping the File menu and selecting New note from template.

4. There's a choice of lined paper, office memo, monthly calendar or To Do List, complete with check boxes to mark off finished tasks.

Above: Write a To Do list, either with your finger or by typing.

5. Create a text box by choosing Insert, then Text box; then write in freehand through the input panel or type using the on-screen keyboard.

6. As the notes are searchable, just use the Search charm to find a particular note later.

Hot Tip

In order to launch Sticky Notes in earlier versions of Windows, go to the Start menu, All Programs, Accessories and select the program.

Sticky Notes

More like the yellow Post-it notes seen in many an office, these can be used for short, quick notes, although you can leave an audio note using the tablet PC's microphone. Open it by typing 'Sticky Notes' in the Search bar on the desktop.

Above: Sticky notes are virtual post-it notes, perfect for writing short memos.

Finger Paint

You can draw with finger or pen using Paint, the illustration program that has been a part of Windows since the beginning. Go to the Search bar and type in Paint to find the Desktop app, and then tap to open it.

There's a refreshed, more artistic version of the app called Fresh Paint, which also lets your fingers do the painting and comes with a number of paid and free art packs with extra features and images to paint.

Weather

Not strictly Windows, but it is pre-installed on Windows tablet PCs and is powered by Bing: Microsoft's search engine. The very dramatic imagery changes to reflect the conditions in your location and it is very easy to operate by touch.

Touch-friendly Apps

- **NextGen Reader**: An RSS (Really Simple Syndication) reader which gathers the latest stories, comments and images from websites, blogs, photo sites, news sites, etc., so you can view them in one place. This reader has a special grid layout designed to suit Modern mode on touch-screen devices.

Above: The OneNote app has a wheel-style menu with various actions.

- **Metro Commander**: A more colourful, easier to use alternative to File Explorer, with dual panes making it simple to move files around.

- **OneNote**: There are two versions of this note-taking app. One is designed for touch and lets you use a pen or your finger to draw in your notes, which are saved to the cloud (in your online storage at OneDrive). The text editor has a novel wheel-style menu for choosing different actions, such as copying, changing font style, and so on. The other OneNote app is part of the full Microsoft Office suite and is for the desktop. You can use both.

- **Fenice for Twitter**: A good way to view your Twitter feed and flip between comments, shared images and web links.

- **TuneIn Radio**: Simple touch operation lets you stream music from radio stations around the world.

- **Wikipedia**: The collaborative encyclopedia is not renowned for its attractive layout, but this touch app is an improvement on the normal way of viewing it through a browser. Information is shown in columns that you can flip through horizontally.

Above: The Wikipedia app allows you to flip through columns of information.

- **Hyper for YouTube**: Lets you stream and download videos in high definition, while also showing the trending videos, most popular and allowing you to save videos to watch later.

Hot Tip

The touch version of Wikipedia is integrated with the Search and Share charms, so you can easily find information, send it to friends and link to it on social networks.

TROUBLESHOOTING
AND MAINTENANCE

TROUBLESHOOTING

When things go wrong, as inevitably they will, there are steps you can take to identify the problems and fix them.

SLOW PC

Like any human, computers aren't always at their best. If your PC seems to be taking much longer than normal to carry out even basic tasks, such as opening a web page or launching a program, there are ways to track the source of the problem.

Check for Malware/Virus

If your PC has suddenly slowed down, there's a strong possibility that it has been infected with malware – either a virus or spyware. You have a fair degree of protection if you turn on Windows Defender, but it's still possible to be infected. In order to check for bugs, open Windows Defender, choose Full in the Scan options and then press Scan now.

If you have commercial anti-malware, then run a manual scan according to the vendor's instructions.

Check Free Disk Space

If you get to the point where you can't download a video file

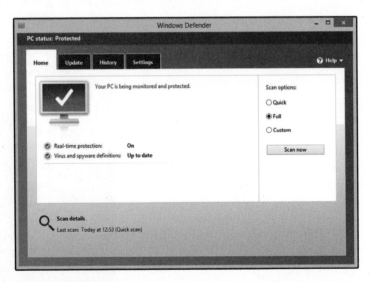

Above: If the PC seems slow, scan for malware to detect any infections.

or there's no space to install the latest killer game, check the amount of available space (*see* page 239).

A quick way to create more space is to add an external drive. Move your large files, which are not accessed often, to the new drive to make more room on your internal drive. Depending on the type of internal drive you have, you should then run a defragmentation program.

Delete Files

An immediate solution is to get rid of the files taking up the most space. Provided you have room to install one, there are hard disk analyser apps, such as WinDirStat or RidNacks, that will scan your system and graphically show the space hoggers so you can remove them.

Check the Hard Drive

The hard drive is one of the PC parts that can fail without notice and cause all sorts of computer errors.

1. If you can still boot into Windows, go to the desktop and open File Explorer. Click This PC, right-click your primary internal drive (normally the C: drive) and select Properties.

2. On the Tools tab, go to Error checking and press the Check button. As Windows monitors the drive in the background, it will tell you if it has found any errors.

Right: Press the Check button under Error checking to scan the hard drive.

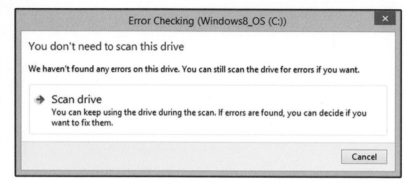

3. Select Scan drive and you can run a manual check. You can carry on working during the scan and will have the option, if any errors are found, of deciding how to fix them.

Hot Tip

While you should never have more than one antivirus program running on your PC, as they'll conflict with each other, you can have more than one anti-spyware program. The theory is that, if one program misses a bug, another might find it.

Check Memory Usage

If your PC slowdown is a gradual process, it may be because your computer is short of memory: the workspace where all your open apps run. The more programs you have open at the same time, the more memory that's used. The latest versions of Windows are very sophisticated at managing this multitasking, but every machine has its limits.

- **Delayed reactions?:** One way to check your machine is to open several larger applications, such as Word or a graphics program, and use Alt + tab to switch between them. If there's a delay in switching or the hard drive is thrashing away, it's likely you need more memory.

- **Restart:** In order to check that it's not just a faulty, memory-hogging program, close all programs and restart to see if that clears the problem.

- **Add more RAM:** If you do need to add more RAM (Random Access Memory is the technical name), see how to do it on page 250.

PC FREEZES OR CRASHES

When it happens, you have no choice but to restart your PC; this often resolves any issues, or at least allows you to explore other troubleshooting methods.

Note Error Messages

These come in various shapes, sizes and places: from the arcane error codes, which are a series of letters and numbers that mean little to anyone except the developers, to full-blown alerts with suggested solutions that are worth trying as a first step.

Check Action Center

Look for notifications by clicking the Action Center icon on the taskbar. In earlier versions a white flag on the taskbar would show a red cross if Windows spotted any problems. In either case, click the alert to see what can be done or where to get more information.

Windows Updates

While it's rare, Windows updates, which happen automatically in the background, can cause problems. You can remove an update, although it is best to do

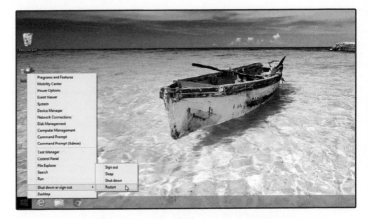

Above: To restart quickly, right-click the Start button and select from the menu shown.

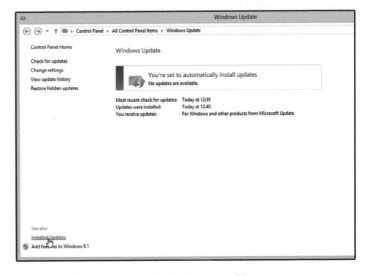

Above: It is possible to remove an update which is causing problems.

this only if advised by a helpline or your computer manufacturer. In order to roll back from a new update, go to the Control Panel, select Windows Update and then Installed Updates from the left-hand panel. Highlight the one you want to remove and click Uninstall on the menu bar.

New Device Added Recently

If you have recently added a new device, turn off and disconnect the devices, then reconnect them and turn them back on to see if that clears the problem.

Check Device Manager

Device Manager will show whether there is a problem with any internal devices.

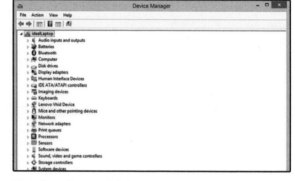

1. Open it by right-clicking the Start button and selecting Device Manager from the pop-up list.

2. Here, you have a comprehensive overview of all your computer's

Above: Device Manager will display warning icons where there are problems.

hardware. There will be one of three different types of warning icon next to devices where Windows has detected there are issues.

- **Black exclamation mark on a yellow background**: Indicates there's a problem with the device. Click on the device and, in the Device Status area, there should be more information about what's wrong and possible solutions.

- **Red X**: Shows the device is disabled or missing.

- **Blue i on white background**: Informs you that the device is not set to Use Automatic Settings but has been changed manually.

Drivers

The majority of problems with devices are due to missing or incorrect drivers (these are small software programs that tell Windows and other apps how to communicate with the hardware).

> # Hot Tip
> Restarting your PC allows Windows to register that a new device has been added and load the drivers.

Step 1: Check next to Digital Signer to see whether the device is signed by Microsoft and has been checked.

Check and Update Drivers

In order to prevent problems, Microsoft digitally signs drivers that they have checked work properly with Windows. It's possible, with older devices, that you may have an unsigned driver. To check your drivers, do the following:

1. Right-click on the device, select Properties and then the Driver tab. Unsigned drivers will have the message Not digitally signed beside Digital Signer. This one is OK, as it's signed by Microsoft.

2. In order to see if there's an update for the driver, which can help resolve problems, click the Update Driver button on the Driver tab.

Step 2: Click the Update Driver button to check for any available updates.

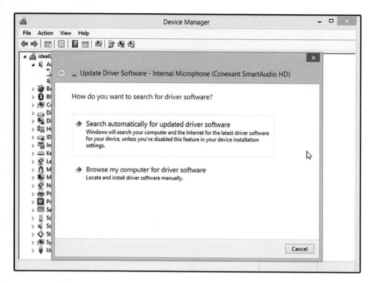

Step 4: Let the computer search automatically for an update, or add one manually.

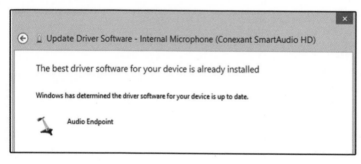

Step 5: The wizard will help you install the latest driver or tell you if it is installed already.

3. This launches the wizard (you can also access this by right-clicking the device name in Device Manager and selecting Update Driver Software).

4. Choose whether to let Windows search your computer and the internet for the best match or add one manually if, for example, you have already gone to the device manufacturer's website and downloaded the latest driver or have a setup disc.

5. If a newer driver is found, the wizard will help you to install it. In this case, the microphone is using the latest driver.

Restore an Old Driver

If it's an updated driver that's causing the problems, try going back to the old one. Do this by using System Restore (see page 173) to revert to a point before the driver was updated. Alternatively, select Roll Back Driver on the Driver tab of the Device Properties box to change only one driver.

TROUBLESHOOTING IF WINDOWS STILL LOADS

If your computer issues are not resolved by other measures, then it's time to let Windows have a go by accessing the loftily named Recovery Environment.

Accessing the Recovery Environment

Go to the Search box, type 'Advanced' and select Change Advanced Startup options from the results. Click the Restart now button and you'll see four options.

- **Continue**: Takes you out of the RE and loads Windows as normal.

- **Use a device**: Lets you use a USB recovery drive or DVD.

- **Troubleshoot**: Contains the main troubleshooting tools.

- **Turn off your PC**: Does just that.

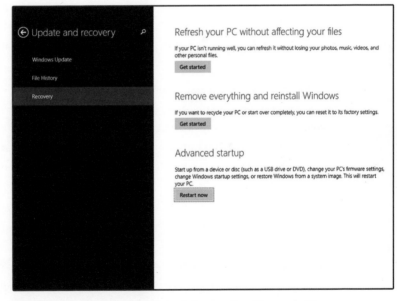

Above: Access the Recovery Environment to refresh, reset or fix problems on your PC.

Recovery Environment

Once you have accessed the Recovery Environment, click Troubleshoot and you can Refresh your PC (*see* page 219) or Reset your PC (*see* page 220). Select Advanced options and you have several problem fixers.

- **System Restore**: Lets you roll back your PC to an earlier time.

- **System Image Recovery**: Uses an image file to recover all the elements of your hard drive.

- **Startup Repair**: Automatically attempts to fix the problems that stop Windows from loading. It will ask for your username and password, and will let you change the keyboard layout. Press Continue.

- **Command Prompt:** This goes back to pre-Windows time and is only likely to be used by support technicians and specialists.

> ## Hot Tip
> In order to boot into recovery mode, in Windows 7, restart your computer and press F8 at startup, then, on the Advanced Boot Options screen, select Repair your computer.

- **Startup Settings**: Changes the way Windows starts up so that you have a chance of resolving problems.

Changing Startup

Among the most useful options for changing the way Windows starts up are the following:

- **Enable low-resolution video mode**: Loads Windows with a low-resolution setting of 640 x 480. This lets you sort out distorted displays by matching screen settings with the capabilities of your video card.

- **Enable Safe Mode**: Loads a stripped-down Windows (*see page 221*).

- **Disable early-launch anti-malware protection**: In case it's the anti-malware scan that's disrupting startup.

Troubleshooting Windows

If you have made any changes in Windows itself – even small ones, such as which apps can send notifications – try reversing them. If you've made a few, you can use System Restore to revert to previous settings when Windows worked well.

System Restore

System Restore points don't cover any of your documents, photos or other data. They allow you to roll back Windows to an earlier time, but any programs and drivers installed since then will be lost. *See* page 173 to see how to use it.

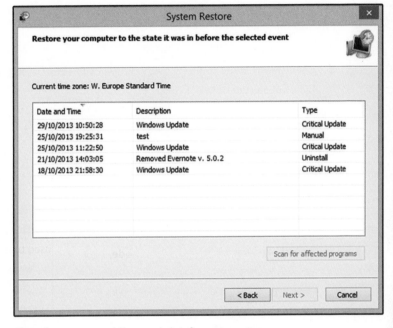

System Restore

Restore your computer to the state it was in before the selected event

Current time zone: W. Europe Standard Time

Date and Time	Description	Type
29/10/2013 10:50:28	Windows Update	Critical Update
25/10/2013 19:25:31	test	Manual
25/10/2013 11:22:50	Windows Update	Critical Update
21/10/2013 14:03:05	Removed Evernote v. 5.0.2	Uninstall
18/10/2013 21:58:30	Windows Update	Critical Update

Scan for affected programs

< Back   Next >   Cancel

Above: Some programs and drivers may be lost after a system restore.

Refresh Your PC

This option lets you reinstall Windows, reverting to its initial settings, while keeping all your data – including documents, photos, music and videos – intact, as well as your user settings. Apps bought through the Microsoft Store are also preserved, but desktop programs, commercial software you've added and browser add-ons will be removed.

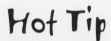

Hot Tip

After Refresh your PC is complete, you'll have to reinstall all third-party software and use Windows Update to reinstall any available operating system updates.

1. On the Start screen, press the Windows key + I to select Settings, Update and Security, then Recovery.

2. Click the link under More recovery options, say Yes to change app and open Fresh Start. Click Get started to begin.

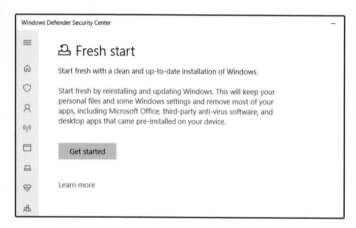

Above: Refreshing the PC allows you to keep your data and user settings intact.

3. A message shows that Windows is preparing the refresh; follow the prompts.

Reset Your PC

This is the back-to-basics option, if all else fails or if you are planning to sell or give away your PC. While your computer will be restored 'as-new', it comes with the removal of all your personal files, apps and programs. All your settings are deleted and restored to their defaults.

1. Access this option, like the Refresh, in the Recovery section of the Update & Security panel.

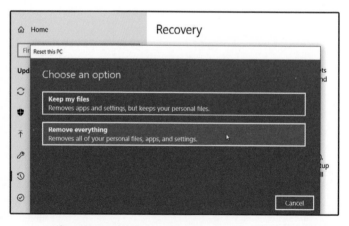

Above: Resetting the PC means all settings will be restored to their defaults.

2. Click the Get started button, choose Remove everything in the pop-up window, then follow the prompts.

TROUBLESHOOTING IF WINDOWS DOESN'T LOAD

If your problems are with Windows itself, such as a buggy driver affecting your monitor, then you can use Safe Mode.

Boot in Safe Mode

This launches the bare essentials Windows, with only the minimum device drivers necessary. In order to remind you that you are in Safe Mode, the words are displayed in the corner.

Once in Safe Mode, you can revert to a previous System Restore Point when Windows was working, roll back or update drivers, or run other troubleshooters.

Use Your Recovery Drive to Access the Recovery Environment

1. Insert the recovery drive in the USB port (*see* page 243 for how to create one).

2. Newer computers will recognize the flash drive automatically and it should appear in the list of available drives in the Use a Device window.

3. Select it, choose a keyboard layout and then, in the Choose an option box, click Troubleshoot.

Hot Tip

Older PCs may have to be told which drive to use to boot up. After you start up, you should see a message about which keys to press to access the Start settings. Follow this and then set your PC to boot from the USB port.

PROGRAM FREEZES

When a program fails to respond to anything you do, like moving the cursor or pressing an option button, Windows will take over and shut it down – but you will probably lose any unsaved work.

Above: Open the Task Manager from the Search bar.

Run Task Manager

This handy tool lets you manage any apps that are running and turn off those that are refusing to quit or not responding. It can be accessed in a number of ways.

1. On the Start screen, type 'Task Manager' and select from the search results.

2. The traditional Windows method is to press Ctrl + Alt + Del and then click Task Manager.

3. On the keyboard, press Ctrl + Shift + Esc.

4. Open the power user menu (also known as Windows Tools Menu) by pressing the Windows key + X and then select Task Manager.

Hot Tip

When Task Manager opens you'll just see a slimmed down version, showing running applications. Click More details for additional information.

Right: Use Task Manager to close a program that is not responding.

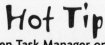

PROGRAMS STOP WORKING

If a program won't launch or crashes soon after it's opened, there are a number of steps to take to get it running again.

Restart the Program and Reverse Any Changes

If you have altered any settings or added different options, try changing these back to see if that resolves the problem.

Run Repair Option

1. Go to Control Panel and click on Programs and features.

2. Highlight the program that you added recently or think may be causing problems.

3. Some programs have a Repair option. If one is available, you'll see a Repair button on the top menu bar. Click this to run the repair.

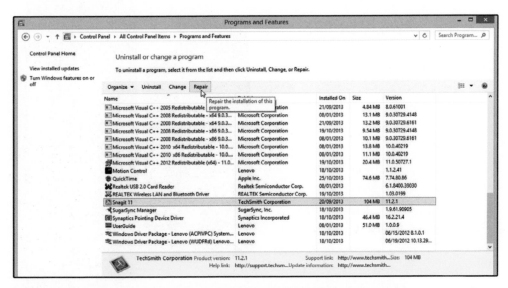

Above: If a Repair option is available for the selected program, a Repair button will appear on the top menu bar.

4. If that doesn't work, or there is no repair option, remove the program by clicking the Uninstall button on the menu bar. If everything now works correctly, you know which app was causing the problems.

Check for Updates

Usually, there is a link within the program to check for updates. It will let you know if one is available and will typically download it for you. If the program won't launch, go to the developer's website to download the new version.

Reinstall the Program

Often, you'll have the choice between a typical install, with the developer-recommended options, or a custom install, where you choose which options you want. If you are having problems with the program, it's probably better to try the typical install, so you can be sure that all the elements are there for the program to run correctly.

SOUND PROBLEMS

Whether you're relying on a built-in speaker or have several for the whole surround sound experience, it's your computer that controls whether you'll hear anything.

No Sound

No sound coming out of your speakers?

○ **Test your speakers:** Right-click the Volume icon (a loudspeaker) in the notification area on the desktop. Choose Sounds, then Playback and Playback devices to see a list of all those available.

Select your speakers and press the Configure button. In the dialogue box that opens, select your setup (e.g. Stereo), click Test and you should hear a musical tone from the left speaker, followed by the right. If you hear the right speaker first, then swap your speakers round.

- **Check the connections**: Make sure that the speakers are plugged into the right port; it's easy to accidentally use the microphone jack.

- **Check the speakers' volume control**: Make sure that it isn't turned down or that the mute button, if there is one, hasn't been accidentally pressed.

- **Check internal volume controls**: There are separate ones for each device that generates sounds. For example, the system sounds that Windows plays, DVD player, etc. If muted, there will be a red circle with a line through it. Right-click the Volume icon in the notification area, select Open Volume Mixer and make sure that none of the devices are muted or have the sound turned down very low.

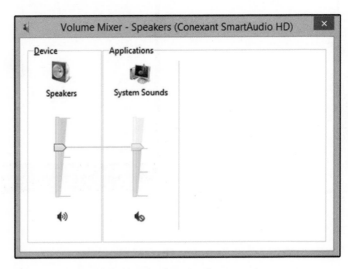

Above: A red circle with a line through it shows the volume is muted.

- **Look in Device Manager**: In order to confirm that there's nothing wrong with your sound card (there will be an exclamation mark if there is).

- **Update the audio drivers**: In case there is a known problem that has been rectified (see how on page 247).

DISPLAY PROBLEMS

Changing monitor screen settings often solves problems, but at times there are real hardware issues.

Snap Apps Not Working

A minimum resolution of 1366 x 768 pixels is necessary to snap two apps to the screen so that they can be seen beside each other at the same time. In order to change the screen resolution, right-click on the desktop and select Screen resolution, and see the maximum possible on your PC or laptop by clicking the drop-down menu beside Resolution.

Above: If snap apps is not working, check the screen resolution is the minimum required.

Hot Tip

The more apps you snap, the higher the resolution that is needed. Currently, it's possible to have up to four applications running at once in Desktop mode but only two in Tablet mode.

Windows Starts in the Wrong View

What constitutes the wrong view will depend on your personal preferences, but these are the options.

- **Tablet mode:** The Taskbar disappears and the app tiles stretch across the screen. Toggle this on and off in the Action Center.

- **Desktop mode:** In desktop view, right-click on the taskbar, select Properties, then the Navigation tab. Select Go to the desktop instead of Start when I sign in.

- **Start screen is too big**: Go to Settings then Personalization and switch off Show more tiles on Start.

No Peeking

Peek lets you see the desktop by hiding open windows when you move your pointer to the bottom-right corner. Click and you go to the desktop. It only works in desktop view and has to be turned on first.

- **Enable Peek**: To turn Peek on, right-click the taskbar, select Settings and toggle on the switch below. Use Peek to preview the desktop when you move your mouse to the Show desktop button at the end of the taskbar.

Taskbar Not Visible

It may be set to auto-hide when not in use. Select the Taskbar tab as above and uncheck the box beside Auto-hide the taskbar.

Screen Items Too Small

You can change the size of text and other items, such as icons, without changing the screen resolution.

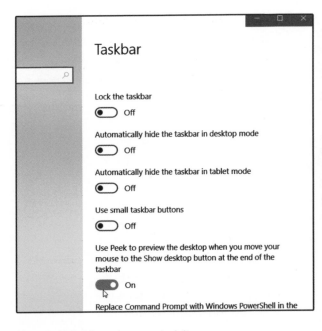

Taskbar

Lock the taskbar
( ) Off

Automatically hide the taskbar in desktop mode
( ) Off

Automatically hide the taskbar in tablet mode
( ) Off

Use small taskbar buttons
( ) Off

Use Peek to preview the desktop when you move your mouse to the Show desktop button at the end of the taskbar
( ) On

Replace Command Prompt with Windows PowerShell in the

Above: Enable Peek for quick access to the desktop.

1. Go to Windows Settings and open Display.

2. Select the size you want in the dropdown menu under Change the size of text, apps, and other items. You may only see the change the next time you sign in.

Screen Won't Rotate

Occasionally, portable screens get stuck in horizontal or portrait mode. In order to unstick them, go to the Control Panel and select Windows Mobility Center. Click the Rotate screen button in the corner of the Screen orientation panel and reset the primary orientation.

Coloured Streaks and Flicker

It might be the first sign that the monitor is failing, but is more likely, particularly with a desktop monitor, to be a simple cable problem. Make sure that the connections are firmly plugged in on both the monitor and PC. In particular, ensure that there's nothing pressing down on the monitor cable that could loosen the connection.

Hot Tip

If your screen is blank, it may just be in Sleep mode, so try waking it up first. If nothing shows, press the monitor's settings button. If the menu appears, the monitor is OK and the problem is with the video card. Check Device Manager for any alerts and solutions.

Hot Tip

In order to close in on just a part of the screen, use the Magnifier tool. Click Settings on the Start screen then go to Ease of Access and select Magnifier. Here you can turn it on and off and change the zoom level.

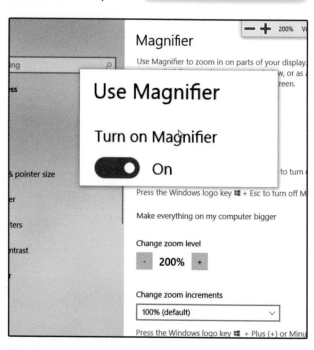

Above: Use the Magnifier tool to zoom in on a particular part of the screen.

BATTERY PROBLEMS

A constant worry for laptop users is how much charge remains on the battery. There are ways to check if your battery is working properly and to conserve energy so you can work on the move for longer.

Check Your Battery

Remove the battery (usually this just slides out from the bottom of the laptop). Plug in the power cord to run it. If it works, it indicates that the battery is defective and should be replaced.

Laptop Won't Start

If the power lamp is on, then there is a hardware problem inside. It's more likely, though, to be a problem with the power supply rather than the battery.

Battery Runs Down Quickly

While Windows comes with several power-management plans, which control settings like brightness level and the period of inactivity before the display shuts off or the computer goes to sleep, you can create your own. Go to the Control Panel, select Power Options and then click Create a power plan in the left panel. You start with an existing plan, give it a name and then alter the settings to suit you.

Fully charged (100%)

Select a power plan:
- ◉ Balanced
- ○ Power saver

Adjust screen brightness
More power options

Above: Keep an eye on how much charge the battery has.

Tips to Conserve Power

1. Create your own custom power plan (as shown here).

2. Manually adjust the brightness level, if possible, to suit the available light.

Above: Create a power plan to save power in a way that suits you.

3. Avoid using power-intensive hardware on your laptop, such as the optical drive, if you have one, and Bluetooth, and switch off Wi-Fi if it's not needed.

4. Mute the sound, which, as well as saving power, means that there are no aural distractions.

Low Battery Warning Comes Too Late

Fortunately, you can adjust this to match your way of working.

1. Go to the Control Panel, select Power Options and then click Change plan settings, which is beside the current power plan that you're using.

2. At the bottom, select Change advanced power settings. This is where you can alter all the energy settings for your hardware and specific situations, such as when you're playing video.

3. Click the + sign beside Battery. From the options, you can change what percentage of charge is left when you get a low battery and critical warning, as well as selecting what action to take – ranging from none to putting the laptop to sleep.

Hot Tip

All batteries get warm when they're in use. However, if it's more than that and is very hot, then it is malfunctioning and needs to be replaced.

PRINTING PROBLEMS

Inevitably, they happen when you're in a hurry and will often involve replacing the ink or toner, but there may be other issues.

Not Printing

First of all, check that the power is on and cables are plugged in.

- **Check ink levels**: Your printer usually comes with a tool that shows how much ink (or toner) you have left. Many inkjets, in particular, are set not to print if there's insufficient ink, as this can damage the printer.

- **Check your default printer**: As well as hardware printers, Windows sets up virtual printers for printing documents to files or programs such as to OneNote. If one of these is

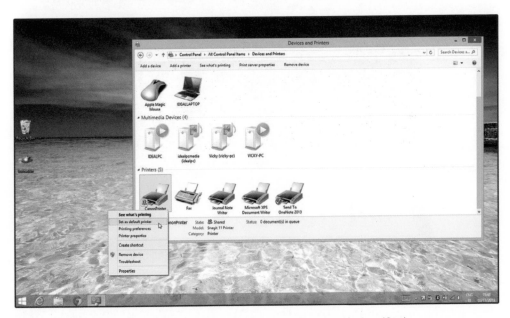

Above: Set up your chosen printer as the default through the Devices and Printers option on the Control Panel.

selected, there'll be no hard copy printout. In order to set your physical printer as the first option for printing, go to the Control Panel, select Devices and Printers, right-click your printer's icon and select Set as default printer.

- **Change or update the printer driver**: The easiest way is to delete the existing printer by right-clicking and selecting Remove device. Then select Add a Printer from the toolbar in Devices and Printers, and follow the wizard to reinstall the printer.

Streaky Print

Unusual or faded colours show that you're running short of ink and need to replace the cartridges (typically, inkjet printers will have one cartridge that contains several coloured inks and a separate one for black ink). If the streaks are down the page, then it may be a leak, with ink having got on to the printer's paper feed.

For a laser printer, the streaks show it's time to replace the toner cartridge.

Misplaced Text on Printouts

If there are odd letters and symbols on the page you have printed, then check that you have the correct printer driver.

1. Go to the Control Panel and select Devices and Printers.

2. Right-click the icon for your printer and choose Printer Properties (not Properties) from the menu.

3. Select the Advanced tab and look at the name next to Driver. This should match your printer name. If it's wrong, then choose the correct one from the drop-down menu.

OTHER SOURCES OF HELP

It's unlikely that your computer problem is unique. Microsoft offers a range of help, including troubleshooters and online support sites, and there are plenty of people willing to share their experience and solutions in online forums.

Windows Troubleshooting Wizards

Accessed by going to the Control Panel and selecting Troubleshooting, there are four main areas of help.

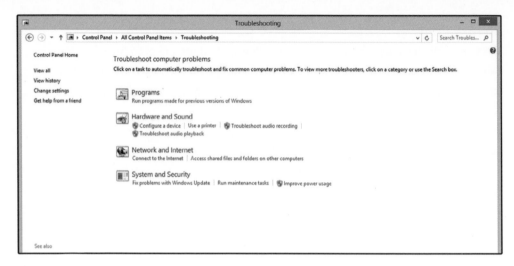

Above: The Troubleshooting wizard will attempt to diagnose and fix different types of problems.

- **Programs:** Lets you run the desktop apps specifically designed for previous versions of Windows by setting up a space for the original operating system in the new Windows OS.

- **Hardware and Sound:** There are separate wizards for configuring a device, using a printer, troubleshooting audio recording and audio playback.

- **Network and Internet:** If you have set up a network and are still having trouble connecting to the internet or sharing files and folders, Windows will attempt to diagnose and fix the problems.

- **System and Security:** Wizards to fix problems with Windows updates, Internet Explorer safety, Windows Search and the power settings, as well as one that runs maintenance tasks.

Windows Help Files

Tap or click the Get Help tile on the Start screen. It links with Microsoft's Virtual Agent online so you get the latest information; however, it does mean that you need internet access to get the most from it.

Forums

These online communities, such as the Microsoft site answers.microsoft.com, are where users and experts share tips and fixes.

Microsoft Support

Access this directly at http://support.microsoft.com. Select your problem area and say what you're trying to do, e.g., Fix performance, errors or crashes, and you can view or run a series of suggested solutions.

Hot Tip

Do a search on any problem you have or error message you've received and you can see where it's being discussed in the many user forums online.

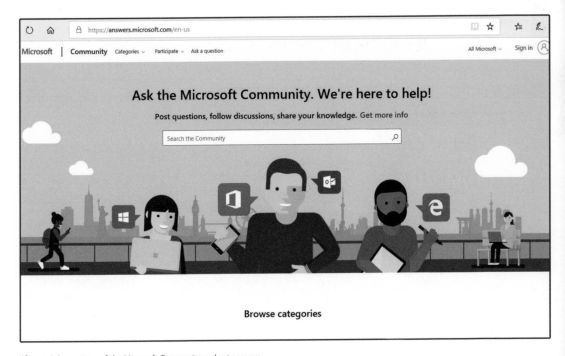

Above: Ask questions of the Microsoft Community and get answers.

REMOTE ASSISTANCE

If you're still up against it, phone a friend or trusted advisor, at least. You give access and control to your computer, via the internet, so they can work out what's wrong and fix it.

Step 2: After typing 'Invite', select the Control Panel option.

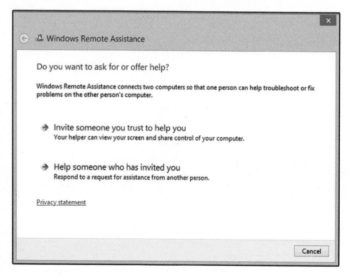

Step 3: Select Invite someone you trust to help you.

Setting up Remote Assistance

1. Type 'Invite' in an empty space on the Start screen (when you do this, Windows automatically opens the Search box and enters the text you're typing into the text box).

2. Select Invite someone to connect to your PC and help you, or offer to help someone else from the results.

3. In the Windows Remote Assistance pop-up, select Invite someone you trust to help you.

4. Save this invitation as a file is the easiest option if you have a webmail account, such as Gmail or Yahoo! You send the invite as an email attachment.

5. Use email to send an invitation works with regular email apps, such as Outlook or Mail.

6. In the Save as dialogue box, name the file, select a location and press Save.

7. Send the invite to your chosen helper. They use the 12-character password they received to initiate a session and try to resolve your computer's problems.

8. You can close the Remote Assistance window at any time to end the connection.

Hot Tip

Remote desktop is different to Remote Assistance. Remote desktop allows you to access your PC wherever you are, via the internet. Remote Assistance lets others access your PC when you're in front of it, to help fix it.

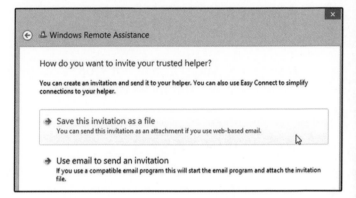

Step 4: The invite can be sent as an email attachment from a webmail account.

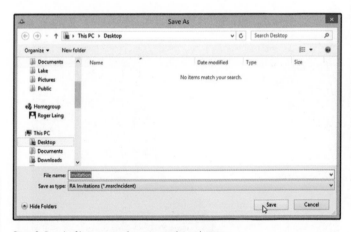

Step 6: Give the file a name and save it to a chosen location.

Step 7: The helper will receive a password in their invitation to start the session.

MAINTENANCE

Maintaining your PC may not stop it crashing, but it will help to avoid some problems and make your computer perform better.

ROUTINE TASKS

Windows performs much of its own maintenance, quietly, in the background. But there are regular tasks you can do to keep it in good shape.

Clean the Screen

1. Disconnect from the power.

2. Touch screens are by their nature likely to need more cleaning than an ordinary laptop or desktop PC. They are very sensitive, as they need to detect touch, so don't use any alcohol or ammonia-based cleaners.

3. The best is a lint-free cloth, which will keep dust and grease off.

4. For heavy duty work, there are monitor-cleaning kits available, which are suitable for desktop and laptop screens.

5. On laptops, make sure that the screen is dry before closing the lid.

Clean the Keyboard

- **Laptop keyboard**: Use a small
  vacuum cleaner to suck up the
  gunge between the keys (don't
  use compressed air to blow, as
  it can just send the dirt further
  down into the machine). When
  cleaning the keys, make sure that
  the laptop is powered down and
  use an eraser to gently rub off the
  accumulated dirt.

- **Standard keyboard**: Unplug before cleaning. Dip a cloth into rubbing alcohol (isopropyl
  alcohol) to clean the tops of keys and surrounding areas.

Check Free Disk Space

While desktop PCs tend to have generous-sized hard drives, with several terabytes of space on
some, laptops and tablet PCs, with the new solid state drives, tend to be much smaller. Here is what
to do to check the available space.

1. Go to desktop mode, open File
   Explorer and select This PC from
   the navigation bar on the left.

2. Select the View tab, then Tiles,
   and you'll see icons for the
   available disk drives. Underneath
   the horizontal bar, you'll see how
   much of the total available space is
   free, e.g., 411 GB free of 439 GB.

Above: Check how much free disk space is available on the computer.

Run Disk Cleanup

This deletes files that are no longer needed. In order to launch it in Windows, go to the Control Panel and, under Administrative Tools, click Disk Cleanup. Check the boxes beside the files you want to remove. There are several options.

○ **Downloaded program files**: Small programs used to run special features on web pages, which are temporarily stored on your hard drive.

Above: Launch Disk Cleanup to delete useless files.

○ **Temporary internet files**: Copies of web pages that you have viewed, which are stored (cached) on your hard drive so they can load more quickly if you decide to go back to them.

○ **Offline web pages**: Copies of web pages that have been downloaded for viewing later when you're not connected to the internet.

○ **Recycle Bin**: Deleted files. They are stored here so that, if you decide you made a mistake, you can fish them out of the bin or, more technically, recover them. It is only when you run this, or right-click the Recycle Bin on the desktop and select the option to empty it, that the files are permanently removed.

○ **Set up log files**: Created by Windows and no longer needed.

○ **Temporary files**: That programs set up while they're running and usually delete when they close. If something happens to prevent that, such as the PC or app crashing, the files get left behind.

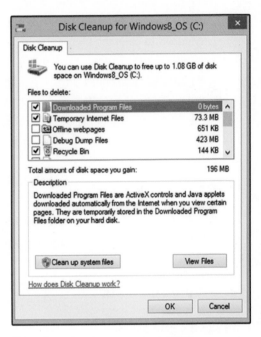

- **Thumbnails**: The images used by Windows to display the small versions of your documents, photos and videos that you see when you browse through your folders. You can delete these and Windows will recreate them as and when needed.

- **Per user archived Windows Error Reports**: Archived copies of the reports that tell Microsoft of problems so they can check for solutions.

Above: Choose from the various options in Disk Cleanup.

Once you've selected the files to remove, press Clean up system files and the app calculates how much space you can save. Click OK to start.

Defragment and Optimize Your Hard Drive

Windows sets itself the task of doing these automatically, on a weekly schedule. In practice, only older mechanical drives are defragmented (that is, where various bits of an individual file, which are scattered all

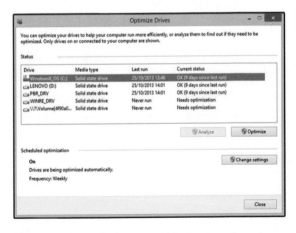

Above: Newer drives can't be defragmented, but are optimized instead.

over your hard drive, are gathered together to be stored in one block. This makes it faster for Windows to open the file).

Newer solid state drives can't be defragmented and this option was turned off in Windows 7. What happens now in Windows is storage optimization: Windows sends 'trim' hints, which let the drive know where files have been moved to or that they have been deleted, so the storage system can clean up the available space before storing any more files.

Hot Tip

It's a good idea to add a description to help you identify any system restore point you create manually. You don't have to add the date and time though, as Windows adds these automatically.

Set System Restore Points

Windows automatically creates system restore points when you install desktop apps and Windows updates, but only if the last restore point was more than a week ago. You can create a manual restore point anytime.

1. Press the Windows key + Break/Pause key and go to Advanced system settings.

2. In the System Properties box, select the System Protection tab and click the Create... button at the bottom.

Easy Access to the Control Panel

The Control Panel has many of the more advanced tools for getting under the hood of Windows and your PC. As such, they are normally buried away. If you plan to run any of them regularly, it's quicker and easier to access them from the Taskbar.

1. In the Search box type Control Panel. When the Desktop app appears, right-click on it.

2. Slide the switch under Show administrative tools to Yes.

Above: You can add the Control Panel to the Taskbar.

RECOVERY DRIVES

These have to be created in the good times when your PC is working well, so that they can be used in the bad times to help you fix your computer, even when it won't start .

Creating a Recovery Drive

Your PC might come with all the files necessary to recover your computer stored on a partition – an area of your hard drive. This recovery partition is fine if your computer starts up well, but, if it doesn't, you should create a recovery drive on removable media, such as a USB drive, DVD or external drive.

1. Insert the drive you want to use. As Windows will erase all data on the drive, make sure that there's nothing on it that you want to keep. It must also be able to hold at least 256 MB.

2. Get started by typing 'Create a recovery drive' in the Search box and' and select it from the results.

3. Work through the wizard, which also gives you the option, if you have a recovery partition, to copy it to the recovery drive so that you can use it to refresh or reset your PC.

4. Once finished, it's a good idea to test whether it works by using the drive to boot up your PC. How this is done depends on your PC.

Right: You can create a recovery drive on an external hard drive, USB drive or DVD.

Recovery Drive

Create a recovery drive

You can use a recovery drive to help troubleshoot problems with your PC even if it can't start. If your PC came with a recovery partition, you can also copy it to the recovery drive so you can use it to refresh or reset your PC.

☑ Copy the recovery partition from the PC to the recovery drive.

Next   Cancel

CREATE A SYSTEM IMAGE BACKUP

If your hard drive and everything with it fails, you will have a mammoth task installing Windows, configuring settings, reinstalling programs and transferring all your data (assuming it's backed up).

Step 2: You'll need to access System Image Backup in the Control Panel.

Step 3: Select System Image Backup from the lower-left corner of the screen.

1. The quick way to do this is to make a regular System Image Backup. This is a complete copy of your hard drive at a given time – in a single image. If the worst happens, or if you're upgrading or replacing your hard drive, you can restore the image and your computer is as it was when the image was created.

2. Introduced in Windows 7, System Image Backup can be found in Backup and Restore (Windows 7) in the Control Panel.

3. In the lower left-corner, select System Image Backup to launch the wizard to create an image.

4. Select where you want to save the backup. There's a warning alert if you try to save it to the same drive that is being backed up.

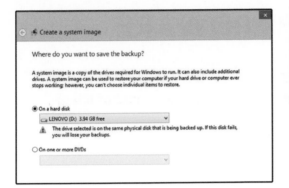

Step 4: Select where to save the backup.

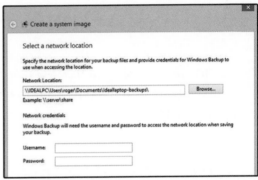

Step 5: Select a network location.

5. Here, a network location is selected.

6. Click Next and choose which drives to include.

7. Click Next and confirm your settings. The prompt box shows how much space is needed – here, it's 46 GB. Click Start backup to create the system image.

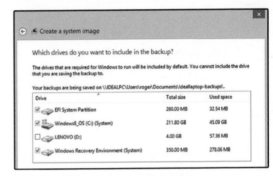

Step 6: Choose which drives to include in the backup.

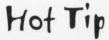

Hot Tip

Once you've completed the System Image Backup, a prompt box asks if you want to create a system repair disk. This is only necessary if you don't have a recovery drive.

Step 7: The promt box will alert you to how much space is needed.

UPGRADING HARDWARE

Just as moving to a new version of Windows changes your PC experience, so adding or upgrading your hardware can bring a new lease of life to your computer.

GETTING STARTED

Preparation helps to make hardware changes go smoothly, and that includes having the right tools and taking the necessary precautions to protect you and your PC.

Tools You'll Need

- **Computer kit**: Should consist of flat-head and Phillips-head screwdrivers, pliers, tweezers and screw grabber. In addition, a torch is always handy, as is an anti-static wrist strap, which has a metal clip at one end that you can attach to a metal object to ground yourself.

- **Computer manual**: To give you the spec for the different parts. If you no longer have it, you can usually find a copy by doing a search online or going to the manufacturer's website.

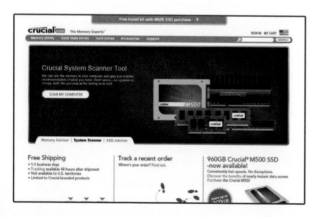

- **System scanner**: If you can't locate the manual, tools like this will automatically gather the information. For example, the scanner from manufacturer Crucial Technology (www.crucial.com) shows the type of memory and hard drive you have, plus compatible upgrades.

Left: System scanner from Crucial Technology.

Before an Upgrade

Before you upgrade any hardware, ensure you have read the following list.

1. Make sure that all your files are backed up – in the cloud or on an external drive.

2. Before you open the computer, check that it is turned off and the power cable is disconnected.

3. Certain parts retain electricity for a while after the power is turned off, so leave some time before you start.

4. Following the manufacturer's instructions, remove the computer's casing or, on laptops, the cover to the part that you want to access.

5. Touch something metal to discharge any static.

Hot Tip

Most modern hard drives come with a Serial Advanced Technology Attachment (SATA) interface.

Above: Anti-static wrist strap.

DRIVES

If you run out of space or want the latest Blu-ray drive for gaming, there's no need to ditch your old PC. Just upgrade the drives.

Installing a New Hard Drive

When you're running out of space for the home movie collection, or your hard drive is failing, you'll need to replace it – which is not as difficult as it sounds. Once inside the case of a desktop PC, the hard drive is easily identified because of its size. Most modern laptops are designed to make it easy to unscrew and slide out the old hard drive and replace it with the new.

○ **Check the spec**: Make sure that the interface, which controls how data travels in and out of the drive, is supported by your computer.

○ **Run System Image Backup**: If your hard drive is still working, this will immeasurably shorten the process of getting your new drive working after installation. See page 244 for how to do it.

○ **Remove the old drive**: Locate the hard drive. Remove the power cable and the interface cable. Be careful not to damage any of the tiny pins inside the connector.

Above: Install the new hard drive into the computer using rails or screws.

- **Release the hard drive from its enclosure**: Typically, it will be held in place by screws, which need to be undone, or with rails either side of the drive, which slide into the slots on the hard drive enclosure. Pull the rails inwards to release the hard drive. Use the same rails with the new drive.

- **Install the new drive**: If the enclosure uses rails, snap them into the holes on either side of the hard drive and slide the drive into the bay. Otherwise, attach the screws. Reattach the interface cable and power supply.

Hot Tip

On older laptops, the hard drive may be underneath the keyboard or even the motherboard, and it is a major disassembly job to reach it.

- **Reinstall Windows**: This could be through a USB recovery drive, network drive or the original Windows installation media.

When you restart the PC, boot to the drive with Windows on it, start the install program and follow the prompts. Restore the content for your hard drive from the System Image Backup made earlier.

Upgrading Optical Drives

The technique is very similar to that for the hard drive: locating the drive, removing the power cable and interface cable, etc. On desktop PCs, rather than replacing an old drive, you may well have an extra bay where you can install your DVD or Blu-ray drive.

Above: Upgrading optical drives is a similar process to upgrading hard drives.

MEMORY

As the workspace for your programs, generally, the more memory you have, the better. This is one upgrade that can make a big difference to your computer's performance.

> ## Hot Tip
> If the hole in the memory module and the central ridge in the socket don't line up, you have the wrong RAM for your computer.

Adding More RAM

- **Check the spec**: Make sure that the memory modules you buy match your system and don't exceed the maximum capacity of your computer. You also need to check (by right-clicking the Start menu and selecting System) whether you're running 32- or 64-bit Windows, as only the faster version can use more than 4 GB of memory.

Above: Slide the RAM module into place.

- **Remove old memory modules**: This step may not be necessary, depending on how many memory slots you have. If you have empty ones, you may be able to simply add the new modules. Locate the memory module you're removing and press down the ejector tabs on the memory socket to move them clear. Then carefully lift the memory module from the socket.

- **Install memory module**: Open the ejector tabs on the socket where you're installing the new RAM. Line up the hole in the memory module with the socket's ridge, then slide the module into the vertical channel on either side of the socket. Press the sockets down and, when they're fully in, the ejector tabs will snap shut.

LAPTOP BATTERIES

Given that this is the most likely part that will need to be replaced on a laptop, the majority of manufacturers make it easy to access – although some, like the Ultrabooks, don't have removable batteries.

Above: Release the attachments holding the battery in place, and slide out.

Replacing a Laptop Battery

1. With the laptop turned off and the power cord disconnected, locate the battery. Typically, it will be on the underside of the laptop.

2. Unscrew or release the attachments securing the battery and slide it out of the compartment. Try not to touch the contacts of the battery itself.

3. Slide the replacement battery into the bay, and secure.

4. Once the power cord is connected, give the battery a full charge.

FURTHER READING

Cisco Networking Academy, *IT Essentials: PC Hardware and Software, Companion Guide*, Cisco Press, 2013

Gookin, Dan, *PCs for Dummies*, John Wiley & Sons, 2015

MacBride, P.K., *Brilliant Home Computer Book: Everything You Want to Do on Your PC When You Want it*, Prentice Hall, 2008

MacRae, Kyle, *Computer Manual: The Step-by-step guide to upgrading, repairing and maintaining a PC*, J H Haynes & Co Ltd, 2010

MacRae, Kyle & Marshall, Gary, *Computer Troubleshooting: The Complete Step-by-step Guide to Diagnosing and Fixing Common PC Problems*, J H Haynes & Co Ltd, 2008

McFedries, Paul, *PCs for Grown-ups: Getting the Most Out of Your Windows 8 Computer*, QUE, 2013

Miller, Michael, *Computer Basics Absolute Beginner's Guide, Windows 10 Edition*, QUE, 2015

Mole, Kenneth, *Easy PC: The computer book that tells you what the others assume you know*, Right Way, 2008

Price, Sue, *Computing for Seniors in Easy Steps*, In Easy Steps Limited, 2013

Smith, Stephie, *BASICS of Windows: The Easy Guide to Your PC*, CreateSpace Independent Publishing Platform, 2013

Wright, Lynn, *Using Your PC Made Easy*, Which? Books, 2011

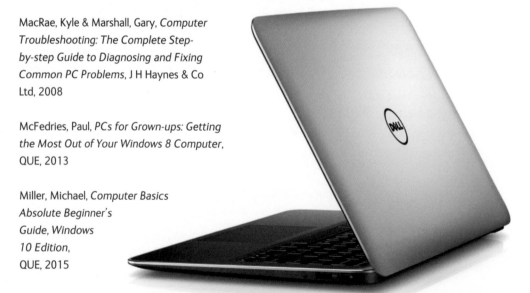

WEBSITES

www.computerhope.com/cleaning.htm

Feel like your PC needs a spring clean?
This site gives lots of information and tips
on how to do so safely.

www.crucial.com

If you are not sure what type of memory and
hard drive you have, head to this site to find out.

www.lifewire.com

Expert-created, real-world technology articles and
tutorials for more than 10 million users.

www.lifewire.com/windows-troubleshooting-4102769

Lifewire's Windows Troubleshooting pages.

onedrive.live.com

Microsoft's cloud service that allows you to store
your files for free.

www.recyclenow.com

If you are upgrading your computer, or any of
your hardware, this site will tell you what to do
with it – don't just throw it in the bin.

www.safenetwork.org.uk

This children's safety site has links to online
safety steps, including helping your children
use social media safely.

strongpasswordgenerator.com

Need a new password? This site will help you
choose a good one.

www.techadvisor.co.uk

Great advice on all things PC: device reviews,
articles, forums and more.

www.techspot.com

A great, general interest site for everything
to do with PCs, with reviews, downloads,
forums and more.

www.truecrypt.org

Site offering free disk encryption software.

which.co.uk/technology/computing

Head for this site for unbiased advice on
buying the computer and related technology
that suits you best.

windows.microsoft.com/en-us/windows/home

Go to this site for help and information on
anything Windows related.

INDEX